Unforgettable Mutts

Unforgettable Mutts
Pure *of* Heart Not *of* Breed

KAREN DERRICO

Foreword by
SUSAN CHERNAK MCELROY

NEWSAGE PRESS

UNFORGETTABLE MUTTS: Pure of Heart Not of Breed

NewSage Press
PO Box 607
Troutdale, OR 97060-0607
503-695-2211 or e-mail: newsage@teleport.com
web site: http://www.teleport.com/~newsage

Book and Cover Design and Production by Karen Derrico

Printed in the United States on recycled paper with soy ink.

Distributed in the United States and Canada by
Publishers Group West: 800-788-3123

Cover Photo: Magic the Dog. Photo © Ron Kimball Studios.
Animal Talent provided by Bow Wow Productions

Page 31, 32: From *Blue Dog* by George Rodrique, with Lawrence Freundlich. Copyright ©1994 by George Rodrique and Lawrence Freundlich. Used by permission of Viking Penguin.

The author has made every effort to obtain and include accurate statistical information as well as proper photo credits and story credits where applicable. Any errors or omissions are unintentional, and therefore not the liability of the author or publisher.

Library of Congress cataloging-in-Publication Data

Derrico, Karen, 1957-
    Unforgettable Mutts: pure of heart not of breed / Karen Derrico;
  Foreword by Susan Chernak McElroy,
            p.   cm.
    Includes bibliographical references.
    ISBN 0-939165-34-1
    1. Mutts (Dogs)--United States--Anecdotes. 2. Mutts (Dogs)-
  -United states. 1, Title.
  SF426.2.D47   1999
  636.7--dc21   99-14107
                                                        CIP

❧ D E D I C A T I O N ❧

In honor of my beloved mutts, Barney and Zelda.
In memory of the millions of mutts who never had the chance for a loving home.
In memory of my father, Dr. Larry Hirsch, who deeply touched my life and so many
other people and animals. In memory of Simba and Caviar, two unforgettable mutts.

ACKNOWLEDGMENTS

The process of putting this book together took me on a much longer journey than I had ever imagined—almost four years from concept to printing press. But the time has served me well. I have met many wonderful people who have inspired me, motivated me, taught me, and supported me throughout this project. To acknowledge them all properly would take an entire book in itself.

First, to my family and friends. My wonderful son, Daniel, and husband Jack, who sacrificed having a mother and wife for many evenings and weekends while I worked on the book, and who were always there to offer love and support. My mother, Harriet Hirsch, who led the way for my lifelong love of animals, and my brother, Steven Hirsch, and sister, Michelle Westin, who were there to lend an ear during the trials and tribulations I endured.

Neighbors, and cherished friends, Susan Allison, Noreen O'Connor, and Kirsten and West Robinson who came to my rescue at a moment's notice with babysitting duty among many other things. Longtime friends and fellow animal lovers, Maria Dales and Lisa Agabian who lent their expertise and moral support.

Anthropologist and author extraordinaire, Mary Elizabeth Thurston, was my guiding light through thick and thin. Mary offered numerous resources and contacts, many good laughs, and sometimes a much-needed shoulder to cry on. She also kindly gave permission to include excerpts from her fascinating book, *The Lost History of the Canine Race*, and to feature several vintage photos from her "museum" of dog artifacts. A good twenty pages of this book I owe to Mary's contributions.

A special thanks to my publisher, Maureen R. Michelson at NewSage Press, for sharing my enthusiasm in this project, and for so carefully and thoughtfully molding the manuscript into a book that I am very proud of.

Thanks also to NewSage copy editor, Tracy Smith, for her fine work and incredible eye to detail. I would also like to acknowledge NewSage Press for publishing this book and several others that will help make the world a much better place for the animals.

Many thanks to Lydia Hiby, longtime friend, animal communicator, and author of the wonderful book, *Conversations with Animals*. Lydia pointed me in the direction of NewSage Press, and has been an enthusiastic supporter of this book and my past publishing projects.

I am deeply grateful and honored to have Susan Chernak McElroy, author of the *New York Times* bestseller, *Animals as Teachers and Healers*, and *Animals as Guides for the Soul*, as the contributor to the Foreword. Her books and words have been an inspiration to me, and have opened the world's eyes to the tremendous impact that animals have in all of our lives.

The most substantial contribution to this book came from the nearly two thousand people who responded to a call for photo and story submissions. To each and every one of you, my heartfelt thanks for your wonderful photos and stories and for your kind notes of enthusiasm and encouragement. None of these stories would have been possible had it not been for more than twenty newspapers that printed my announcement calling for submissions. Thank you to all who participated.

Ellen Chang, creator of the wonderful Joy of Mutts web site, so generously dedicated and created an entire page on her site for a book naming contest, voting poll, and a photo and description of the book—thank you.

Other individuals and organizations I would like to acknowledge for their contributions and support include: John Dommers at HSUS, Paul Glassner, and the San Francisco SPCA, Debbie Frazier at Dogs for the Deaf, Paul Jolly at Petco Stores, Terri Crisp and Samantha Glen, authors of *Out of Harm's Way*, Jane Lidz, author of *Zak: The One-of-a-Kind Dog*, Gretchen Wyler at The Ark Trust, Mary Brankovic, and the SPCA Los Angeles, Paws with a Cause, Ann Sellaro, Frank Inn, George Rodrique, Carey Wiggins at AHA, and Jessie Vicha of McDowell and Piasecki.

Last, but certainly not least, I want to thank my very own unforgettable mutts, Barney and Zelda, who were my main inspiration for this book, and who spent countless hours and many late nights curled up on my office floor while I worked.

Contents

Foreword

*I*t has been a long time—too long—since I have revisited my warmest memories of my beloved mutts. However, after reading Karen Derrico's book, *Unforgettable Mutts*, I reminisced on the purest and simplest joys I have had with dogs. In reading about other mutts and their people, I found myself basking in the wonder of a dog's devotion, joy, and wordless companionship. The most priceless power of a person's story is its ability to evoke remembrances for others. This thoughtful and heartfelt celebration of "muttdom" will call forth treasured memories for anyone who has ever given her or his heart to a mutt.

My first mutt, Keesha, was my animal companion for nearly eleven years. Keesha, a shepherd and malamute mix, was, I thought, from the best of all possible dog worlds. She brought me the devotion of her shepherd ancestry, the independence of her sled-dog heritage, and the unique beauty of blended breeds. A mutt myself of German and Czechoslovakian ancestry, I brought to Keesha my solid Teutonic heritage, spiced with a wild dash of Hungarian gypsy—my grandmother's gift to me. Keesha and I were partners—no word describes our union better.

When Keesha died, it was eleven years before another dog began calling to me again. At first, I dreamt about her. She showed herself over and over in my dreams, clear as spring water, vivid as autumn, so that I would recognize her instantly in waking time. She was a collie and shepherd mix, and maybe something else. Brown and furry beyond belief with eyes like brown topaz. Her name would be Arrow. Four months later, she made her appearance at an animal shelter. She was one of five skinny puppies rescued from a pier in Seattle. When I walked into the room she stood up and looked squarely at me. I burst into tears in that moment of recognition.

Today, Arrow rests at my feet as I write. She is six years old and in her glorious prime. We have another dog, too, Strongheart. He is a purebred Anatolian Shepherd who protects our family, but it is Arrow, the mutt, who remains the guardian of my soul.

Unforgettable Mutts is more than a validation to those of us who have loved mixed-breed dogs. It is also an important testimony against prejudice. This fascination we humans seem to have with blood purity, breeding, and origins has been a root cause of the suffering of millions of living beings, human and animal.

I question this notion of blood purity at the canine level as well as at the human level. I remember some of the challenges my parents faced with our first two family dogs, Lady and Sugar, who were purebreds. Lady was crippled by hip dysplasia when she was only six months old. Sugar, at eight months, had been shuttled to four different homes because she did not live up to her show-dog potential. She was a coal-black shepherd and her color was not prized in the show ring back then.

Strongheart, my current purebred dog, has been diagnosed with a peculiar auto-immune disorder, and his back legs are not strong. There is no question in my mind that these three dogs of mine have suffered just a few of the consequences of being pure of breed.

Often, I have wondered, What has happened to us? Why are our hearts so hardened and our vision so corrupted with shallow appearances and a false image of value? How can people learn to see the worth, the vitality, and the enormous heart of the mutt?

Certainly, Karen Derrico sees the mutt's soul. Her devotion to a dog's "purity of heart" is evident in her writing. Her enthusiastic effort on behalf of these enchanting and devoted animals is admirable. *Unforgettable Mutts* so overflows with the essence of the pure heart and the nobility of the mixed-blood, that mutt owners everywhere will have to take precautions to keep themselves from bursting with pride.

The next time you are called to find an animal companion, sit down and re-read this very special book that you hold in your hands. Then, go search for that one-of-a-kind mutt that the universe will never see again.

—*Susan Chernak McElroy*, BRIGHTSTAR FARM

Ode to a Mutt

Born in an alley, one of six was I,
No right to live, too tough to die.
Worn out mother, father unknown,
Runt of the litter, in a world alone.

Raised in the streets by wits alone,
Taken in twice by what I hoped was home.
Not well bred the people would say,
Can't keep him when he looks that way.

Legs too long, head too small,
Didn't notice the heart at all.
Look at me deep I wanted to say,
I'll give you love, please let me stay.

Somewhere I know there's a place for me,
Where I can share love someone will see.
Someone will look beneath my fur and skin,
See my soul and take me in.

—ANONYMOUS

Introduction

THE "UGLY MUTT" STORY

"That dog is so ugly, and he's *just* a mutt! I want a purebred dog. You know, like a German shepherd or a collie." Those were the words of my husband, Jack, when I brought our first dog, Barney, home from the animal shelter. I'll never forget that day. It was August 1988, we had been married less than a year, and had just moved into our first house in Southern California. Adding a dog to our household was probably the last thing on Jack's mind, and the first thing on mine.

I have always loved dogs, and had grown up with several, but was unable to have pets in the apartments I lived in before getting married. I visited my mother frequently to get my "dog fix" from Simba, Caviar, and Chloe (all mutts), but still longed to have a dog of my own.

About a month after moving into our house, I was driving home from work one day, when all of the sudden it was as if my car switched to auto-pilot. The next thing I knew, I was pulling into the parking lot of the local animal shelter. Amazingly, I had never actually been to an animal shelter before, since all of the dogs I had as a child were brought home by my parents. I wasn't sure what to expect, and wasn't sure how I ended up there, but without a moment's hesitation, I hopped out of the car and headed straight for the entrance.

There were only a few dogs at the shelter that day, but once I saw Barney I knew why I ended up there on this particular day. He looked like a cross between Benji and Tramp (the dog from the movie *The Lady and the Tramp*), and had such a loving, happy-go-lucky disposition. When I took him out to the play area, we bonded instantly.

He was about a year old, and was brought in by a woman who found him wandering the streets, covered in chewing gum and dirt. She wanted to keep him, but was living in a small apartment, and already had another dog. The shelter manager told me that the woman was crying

Photo by Karen Derrico

Barney

hysterically when she brought Barney in, concerned that he might not be adopted, and may have to be euthanized. Since I knew I was adopting him, I asked for her phone number to let her know that Barney had found a good home. Then I filled out the adoption paperwork, and Barney and I were on our way.

On the drive home I was nervous anticipating how Jack would react. As soon as we walked through the door, Barney ran directly over to Jack as if he'd known him all his life, his tail wagging furiously, and smothering him with kisses. Surely I thought Jack would fall instantly in love—boy was I wrong! That night Barney and I camped out together on the living room floor because Jack refused to allow him in the bedroom. And the next morning, Jack insisted that I take Barney back to the shelter because he didn't want a mutt. But after a few hours of pleading, I finally convinced him to give Barney a chance.

By the end of the first week, Barney was sleeping on our bed (sometimes under the covers), and soon thereafter, Jack was referring to him as his "kid." Over the next several months I watched with great joy as their bond grew deeper. The dog that Jack initially referred to as an "ugly mutt," had become the most wonderful dog in the world to him. Fortunately, since Barney had already paved the way, things went a lot smoother when I adopted our next mutt, Zelda, a few years later.

Barney, Zelda, and all of the dogs in this book are lucky—they were given the chance that millions of other mutts may never have. According to The Humane Society of the United States, approximately 75 percent of all dogs entering animal shelters each year are mutts. Although some are adopted, between one and two million mixed-breed dogs are euthanized. People are often hesitant to adopt a mutt because they are not sure what personality traits the dog will have, or they are under the common misconception that if a dog is not purebred, he or she must be somehow defective. This, of course, could not be further from the truth.

But the main problem facing all dogs in this country—whether mutts or purebreds—is the pet overpopulation crisis. Between two to four million dogs are sadly destroyed in animal shelters each year. One of the main causes for this horrible statistic is pet owners who do not spay or neuter their dogs. In just six years, it is estimated that one unspayed female dog and her un-neutered and unspayed offspring can produce up to 67,000 puppies. Adopting a dog is saving a life, but if the dog is not immediately spayed or neutered, many other dogs will perish, simply because there are not enough homes for them.

ABOUT THIS BOOK

It has always bothered me that mutts are considered the outcasts of the dog world, but it really hit home after we adopted Barney and Zelda. Many people would stop us, and still do, to ask what type of dogs they are. When we tell people they are mutts, the typical response is usually "oh really," punctuated with a disappointed facial expression and tone of voice. After realizing that Jack was not the only one who had a terrible misconception about mutts, I became determined to do something about it.

I started a regional pet magazine in Orange County, California called *Pet Gazette*, featuring photos and descriptions of pets for adoption at neighborhood animal shelters. Barney even had his very own column, "Dear Barney," where readers wrote in with questions about their pets. Many dogs were adopted as a result of my magazine, but I knew I had a long way to go. There were still millions of homeless mutts across the United States, and millions of people who needed convincing about how wonderful these dogs really are.

Thinking of everything short of going on the "Oprah" show to get the word out, I decided a book would provide the best publicity for mutts on a national level. I sent a press release and a photo of Barney to newspapers nationwide, calling for photos and stories about mixed-breed dogs for my book. More than twenty newspapers ran my article, and I received nearly two thousand submissions from mutt lovers coast to coast.

There were so many wonderful stories and photos, it was extremely difficult selecting which ones to include in the book. But after several months of poring through submissions, I finally narrowed it down to a strong representation of the millions of magnificent mutts across America.

The result, *Unforgettable Mutts: Pure of Heart Not of Breed*, is a celebration and tribute to mutts past and present. Shadow, the scuba diving labrador mix; Josh the "Wonder Dog" who ran for U.S. President; Owney, the U.S. postal mascot who traveled around the world; Ginny, a terrier mix who rescues abandoned cats; and Runway, who gets around in a canine "wheelchair," are just a few of the inspiring and heartwarming tales inside this book.

But this book is not just about mutts—it's also about the caring people who have taken these special dogs into their homes and hearts. During his presidency, Lyndon Johnson took in a small white stray named Yuki, who was his constant companion at the White House; Hollywood animal trainer, Frank Inn, rescued the famous Benji from a Los Angeles animal shelter; and Nipper, the RCA mascot was rescued from a medical research lab by the Dawn Animal Agency. Most of the people in this book, however, are not famous celebrities or presidents—they're just every day people with extraordinary hearts who have recognized that "beauty is more than fur-deep."

If you are not a mutt owner, but are considering adopting one, hopefully this book will convince you to consider a mixed-breed dog. The Resources section includes listings for several pet adoption web sites and recommended books to assist you in your search for a marvelous mutt or purebred dog, as well as listings on a wide variety of dog-related resources—from fun activities and contests to mutt clubs and more.

It is my hope that *Unforgettable Mutts* will give mixed-breed dogs the long overdue recognition they deserve. I love all dogs, whether mutts or purebred, but most importantly I believe that *every* dog deserves an equal chance for a loving family and a place to call home, regardless of heritage. The dogs and people in this book offer us an essential lesson about unconditional love. As Jane Lidz, author of *Zak: The One-of-a-Kind Dog*, so perfectly expressed it, "We are all one of a kind, yet we are all one."

A young boy proudly poses with his mutt during the height of canine discrimination in the early 1920s.

CHAPTER ONE

Canine Discrimination

HOW IT ALL BEGAN

When you stop and think about it, most of us are "mutts." The vast majority of the world's human population comes from a blended lineage, and the same applies to the world's canine population, including the dogs we refer to today as "purebred." So what started this crazy notion that purebred dogs are "better" than mutts? And just how did the purebred dog craze come to be?

In a fascinating book, *The Lost History of the Canine Race*, anthropologist Mary Elizabeth Thurston goes into great detail about the evolution of the purebred versus mutt mentality. According to Thurston, it started in the 1800s. During this time, "sweeping social and economic reforms began to take place in industrialized Europe and America," which dramatically altered the lives of people and dogs. As the standards of living were raised, so were the standards for what types of dogs were deemed as worthy or acceptable.

"The 'fancy'—selective breeding of dogs—first began as a popular form of recreation, not just for aristocracy, but for the middle class, as they aspired to gain higher social status." In the early 1800s dogs were categorized by function rather than physical appearance. "Beast Dog," "Coach Dog," and "Vermin Dog," were a few of the terms used to label a wide variety of dogs. By 1850, though, controlled breeding was deemed necessary in order to create a more refined canine population composed of "superior specimens."

According to Thurston, "The quest to eliminate cosmetic physical differences in dogs of the same variety inspired a new definition of the term 'breed,' which was now used to label dogs of like appearance, rather than function. Dog fanciers welcomed the imposition of human social concepts on the canine race as an improvement of nature; the further removed dogs became from their wild origins, the better off they would be. Not only would their health and beauty improve, but their morals and intellect as well."

"No one would plant weeds in a flower garden, so why have mongrels as pets?" asked George Taylor, in his book *Man's Friend the Dog*, written in 1891. In his expert opinion, mixed-breeds were "mischief loving," and had "dirty tendencies." Victorian dog expert, Gordon Stables, echoed the same sentiment. "Nobody who is now anybody can afford to be followed about by a mongrel dog," he wrote, reflecting middle-class dreams of the good life. As is still common practice, a person's social status was then labeled by his possessions, including the type of dog he owned.

As we closely follow the lives of the British royals today, including their canine companions, it was no different in the reign of Queen Victoria from 1837 to 1901. Her love for dogs was well known by everyone. The royal kennel was always full, housing everything from foxhounds and staghounds to tiny pomeranians. "The Queen's affinity for dogs, blended with the middle-class fantasies of higher social status, fueled the market for pedigreed dogs," writes Thurston. This of course continued to heighten the regard for mutts as worthless "street curs."

The demand for purebred dogs began to increase dramatically, and breeders were cashing in on the opportunity. "Clinging to traditional class separations, many 'pedigreed' people believed that breeding of 'blue-blooded' dogs should remain in the hands of nobility, so impeccable canine lineages would not be soiled by profiteers. Despite this, middle-class dog breeders remained enthralled by the prospect of rubbing shoulders with society's finest," writes Thurston. In fact, middle class breeders and enthusiasts eventually overwhelmed aristocrats in positions of power within the dog fancy.

In an effort to perpetuate an aura of glamour, methods for documenting a dog's ancestry became very important. Strict guidelines for purebred dog registration were imposed in order to not only exclude certain animals, but also certain people, mostly foreigners and the lower class. "The dream of a canine hierarchy became increasingly complex, with dogs being repeatedly recategorized or split into more specialized groups as the number of dog owners

© Collection of Mary E. Thurston

A woman and her mutt, circa 1900.

swelled. Increasingly, dogs were being defined by appearance alone," and not for behavioral traits.

While all of this was going on, mutts were still being regarded as the rejects of the dog world. Like their owners, they were considered "miserable, degenerated animals, cast off by the better classes," wrote Alfred Brehm in his children's periodical, *Brehm's Lives of Animals*. But nevertheless, the show must go on. And so it did. In 1859, the first structured dog show competition was held in Britain at Newcastle-on-Tyne. Sixty hounds entered in competition, divided into two broad classes for pointers and setters. The show was a huge success, and marked the beginning of the dog show as we know it today, but a lot less civilized.

In following years there were numerous reports of corruption and poor sportsmanship in the show world, and some serious "dog fights," between both people and dogs. In 1873 the British Kennel club was established to function as a registry and a union of sorts, lobbying on behalf of the breeding industry, and in 1884, the American Kennel

Club (AKC) was founded.

A lot has changed in the dog world during the past century. The AKC's list of recognized breeds has swelled to 150, and now there are hundreds of fancy dog shows each year like Westminster, and the Cruft's dog show in Britain.

At the onset of the twenty-first century, many people still maintain the old Victorian mentality of purebreds versus mutts—that a dog isn't a "real dog" unless he or she has a pedigree. Hence the main reason for this book—to prove once and for all, that it's a dog's personality, not the pedigree, that really matters!

HOW PUREBRED DOGS HAVE SUFFERED

The popularity of breeding, owning and showing pedigreed dogs has resulted in some tragic side effects for the canine race. Purebred dogs as well as mutts have suffered greatly. The inception of the AKC in 1884, and the growing popularity of dog show competitions, put increasing pressure on breeders to produce "champion-quality" dogs. When a pup or litter was born with a few hairs out of place, or other minor imperfections, the puppy was destroyed like a piece of defective merchandise.

Although things have come a long way, unfortunately there are still some breeders who euthanize dogs for unnecessary reasons. They see dogs strictly as money-making machines, not as the thinking, feeling and loving beings that they are. If they can't get top dollar, then the dog just isn't worth their trouble.

Worst of all are "backyard breeders" or "puppy mills," who breed dogs in horrendous conditions just to make a buck. Dogs are cramped in filthy cages, barely fed or cared for, and often become seriously ill or die as a result. The dogs that do survive are sold to people through newspaper ads or retail pet stores. In many cases, the new owners are burdened with substantial vet bills after the dog begins to display symptoms of various diseases or illnesses they contracted due to improper care.

A *Time* magazine cover article in December 1994, titled "To the

Dogs, the Shame of Overbreeding," goes into detail about how the "obsessive focus on show-ring looks is crippling, sometimes fatally, America's purebred dogs." The article states that as many as 25 percent of the twenty million purebred dogs in America—one in four animals—are afflicted with a serious genetic problem. A few examples include: German shepherds—who have a high risk of hip dysplasia (a condition that deteriorates the hip socket); labrador retrievers are prone to dwarfing; the majority of collies suffer from genetic eye problems; dalmations are often born deaf; and great danes have weak hearts.

"Who is to blame for the shabby treatment of humanity's best friend?" *Time* asked. "The AKC with its focus on pedigrees and beauty pageants, rather than canine well-being? Legitimate breeders, who supply customers with beautiful but sometimes damaged puppies? Puppy mills, which do the same but at much higher volume and greater profits? Or the public, more insistent with each passing year that a mutt—a 'randomly bred dog,' to be politically correct, simply won't do?"

According to veterinarian Michael W. Fox, a Vice President of The Humane Society of the United States, the AKC is a major contributing factor to the health deterioration and exploitation of purebred dogs. In an interview for the *Time* article, Fox stated: "The best use of pedigree papers is for housebreaking your dog. They don't mean a damn thing. You can have an immune-deficient puppy that is about to go blind and has epilepsy, hip dysplasia, hemophilia and one testicle, and the AKC will register it."

Animal welfare advocates point out that the main reason puppy mills continue to thrive is because the AKC allows breeders to register dogs by the thousands, sight unseen. Despite a weak-voiced disclaimer issued recently by the AKC, that little certificate is interpreted by the public as an implication of superior quality. Pet stores depend on AKC papers to justify charging hundreds of dollars for mass-produced dogs, and to date the AKC refuses to limit the number of dogs it will register. Pupppy registrations generate millions of dollars per year for the AKC, and incredibly they are a registered tax-exempt organization.

Photo by Andrew Forsyth © RSPCA, England

Jake, winner of 1998 Scruffts "Dog of the Year" award in England.

Another problem the purebred dog craze has created is the impulse purchase of certain breeds after the release of a TV commercial or series featuring a particular breed, or movies like *101 Dalmations, Beethoven,* and *Lassie.* People rush out to get the dog of the moment without doing any homework to find out if the dog is suitable for their family or lifestyle. As a result, animal shelters are flooded with whatever breed was featured in the movie or commercial once the novelty wears off. As I'm writing this, the current dog of the moment is the Taco Bell chihuahua.

But what about mutts? After all, this book is about mutts, not purebred dogs. The good news is that the acceptance of mutts has increased dramatically over the past few decades. In fact, nearly half of an estimated 32 million dog owning households in the U.S. have mutts, and the majority of British dog owners share their homes with mongrels (their term for mutts). Ironically the British—who were originally responsible for fueling the purebred dog craze—now hold an annual dog show called "Scruffts," which only allows mongrels❧

Owney, U.S. Postal Mascot 1888—1897

CHAPTER TWO

Famous and Historic Mutts

*A*lthough not always as highly publicized as their purebred counter-parts, thousands of mutts have made their marks in history. If this chapter included all of the famous and historic mutts, it would take up several volumes in itself. Some of history's most memorable mutts are profiled on the following pages.

◆ ◆ ◆

Owney
WORLD'S MOST TRAVELED DOG

On a cold winter night in 1888, a lonely stray dog seeking shelter and warmth wandered into the Albany, New York post office through a small opening. Once inside, he found an inviting pile of soft empty mail bags where he curled up and drifted off to sleep.

Postal clerks arriving the next morning were quite surprised to find the little brown mutt. But his pleading look and charming manner easily persuaded them to let him stay. Several days passed, and no one turned up to claim the dog. By this time the postal clerks had grown quite attached to him, and voted to adopt him as their post office mascot. They named him Owney.

After his first night in the post office, Owney seemed to think of any mail bag as his own. In those days, mail was transported daily by horse-drawn wagons to a local train depot, and then distributed by railway around the country. Each day Owney waited eagerly until the last mail bags were loaded on the wagon, then jumped aboard to personally escort the mail to and from the train station. He rode sitting atop the pile of mail bags as if he were standing guard.

Owney began traveling with the mail bags wherever they went. He rode the railways, jumping from one train to the next, and soon made friends with hundreds of postal workers in places he visited around the country. The railway clerks loved having Owney aboard, and always made sure that he was warm, safe, and well fed. There were frequent train derailments and collisions in those years, but no train that Owney traveled on was ever in an accident, thus earning him the reputation as the railway clerks' "good luck charm."

Owney's Albany post office family became concerned that he might get lost during his travels, so they fitted him with a special collar and tag bearing his name and the address of their post office. On the collar they posted a note asking postal clerks in other places he visited to add tags to show that Owney had been there. Eventually he collected so many tags that his collar could no longer hold them all. When U.S. Postmaster General John Wanamaker heard about the dilemma, he ordered a special harness-like jacket for Owney that could hold all of his tags.

By the time he "retired," Owney had collected a total of 1,017 tags. Several of the tags were coin-like tokens given to him by special friends. One read "Good for one drink or cigar," from H.J. Thyts of Reno, Nevada, and another token was "Good for 5¢ Trade or Cash" at D.C. Brenner and Company in Louisville, Kentucky. Other tokens he acquired read: "Good for a 5¢ loaf of bread" from a baker; "Good for 5¢ at the bar" from Logan, Ohio; "One quart of milk" in Nashville, Tennessee; and "Good for 25¢ in furniture" at a dry goods store in Pontiac, Illinois.

Owney made thousands of friends during his travels and each trip was an exciting new adventure for him. In all, he logged a total of 143,000 miles. His most remarkable trip took him all the way around the world, earning him the title of "The World's Most Traveled Dog."

His journey began in Tacoma, Washington in August 1895. With a tiny suitcase, containing his sleeping blanket, brush, and comb, Owney boarded the steamship *Victoria*, bound for Japan. He was sent registered mail part of the way, so postal clerks created a special mail classification that read: "Registered Dog Package." After arriving in Japan, he was introduced to the emperor who added a tag to his jacket. His next stop was China, and during his trip back home, he collected medals in Singapore, Hong Kong, Port Said, and Algiers. His world tour took 132 days. When Owney arrived back in Tacoma, Washington, hundreds of postal workers turned out to welcome him home.

In 1987, after nine years of traveling, Owney's Albany postal worker family decided it was time for their beloved mascot to retire. By that time, he only had one good eye, and could eat nothing but soft foods. One of his last trips was to San Francisco to attend the annual convention for the National Association of Railway Clerks. During the meeting, Owney was brought up on stage where he stood before thousands of postal friends who cheered and applauded during a fifteen-minute standing ovation.

After returning to the Albany post office to live out his retirement days, Owney soon became restless. In June 1897 he slipped out and boarded a mail train bound for Toledo, Ohio. There he passed away surrounded by postal workers who knew and loved him. But Owney was not quickly forgotten. U.S. postal clerks collected money for his preservation by a Toledo taxidermist. Owney was first exhibited at the Post Office Department's headquarters in Washington, D.C., and in 1911 he was given to the Smithsonian Institution. Owney now has a permanent home at the Smithsonian Postal Museum, where he is displayed wearing his famous jacket with all of the tags ❧

Schwinden Library—Montana Agricultural Center

Shep

THE MOST FAITHFUL MUTT IN HISTORY

Throughout history there have been many stories about dogs' love and devotion to humans, but none more remarkable than the heart-wrenching story of Shep, a dog who sat vigil, grieving for his dead owner for five and a half years.

Shep's saga began in the 1930s, in the small town of Fort Benton, Montana. Conductor Ed Shields worked for the Great Northern Railroad, which made daily stops in Fort Benton bringing passengers from nearby towns. One day in August 1936, he noticed a stray dog waiting by the side of the train as passengers unloaded. He watched as the dog looked eagerly at each passenger, wagging his tail and sniffing the air to catch their scent. It was as if he was expecting to see someone he knew. When everyone disembarked from the train, the dog hung his head, lowered his tail, and laid down to rest beside the tracks.

This same routine continued for several days. Shields began to question local townspeople about the dog, but no one seemed to know anything. One morning, as the train pulled into the station, a passenger from a nearby town immediately recognized the dog. He told Shields that the dog belonged to a sheepherder named Ray Castle who had died a few weeks earlier.

Apparently the dog, later named Shep, had been sitting vigil for several days outside a nearby hospital where his owner lay dying. The day after Castle's death Shep followed closely behind the casket as it was carried to the Fort Benton train station. He stood off to the side and watched, sadly whimpering, as his lifelong friend, the sheepherder, was loaded aboard and sent off to a cemetery in the East. Thus began one of the longest and saddest vigils by a dog ever witnessed.

Shep waited, day after day, meeting four trains daily as they pulled into the station. He waited anxiously as each passenger stepped down onto the platform, hoping that one would be his beloved friend. Shep took up residence under the platform, where he had dug himself an area to sleep. Several employees of the railway made sure that he always had food, water, and blankets to keep him warm. But he would not let anyone get close enough to pet him, until several years later. He rarely wagged his tail except when he heard a train whistle—always hopeful that the approaching train would be carrying the one man that he so desperately missed.

After a few years of the daily vigils, Shep's incredible story began appearing in local newspapers. Almost overnight, the word spread throughout the country and around the world. Articles appeared in *The New York Times, The London Daily Express*, and *Reader's Digest*. Mail poured in addressed to Shep, and dog lovers everywhere sent gifts of food and money to help care for him. People began traveling from long distances to see Shep, and many wanted to adopt him. Train passengers would hang out of the windows at the station just to get a glimpse of him.

As time passed, Shep grew to accept people's adulation. He would allow people to pet him and give him food, but followed no one. It was clear that he wanted to be nowhere else but there at the train platform, waiting for Ray Castle to return. During his later years Shep finally accepted an invitation to sleep inside the train depot by the fireplace. His joints were stiffening and the cold made it more difficult to move about.

As Shep got older, he became hard of hearing, which is what so tragically took his life. On a cold winter morning on January 12, 1942, Shep failed to hear the train whistle of old number 235 as it approached the station. He turned to look when the engine was almost upon him, moved to get out of the way and slipped on the icy rails. After five and a half long years of waiting, Shep would finally be reunited with his human companion.

The following day, the news of Shep's death was carried over the wire services. Thousands of people mourned his loss and hundreds of townspeople and dignitaries attended his tearful funeral ceremony. He was laid to rest on the bluff overlooking the station where his long wait had been in vain. Boy Scouts were his pall bearers and the service closed with "Eulogy of a Dog," read by Senator George Graham Vest.

In 1992, on the fiftieth anniversary of Shep's death, the Kiwanis Key Club held a memorial service to commemorate his passing. Included in the service were those who participated in the original burial rites, and those who preserved Shep's story were recognized. Once again, Shep became famous. His story spread to the wire services and to CNN for worldwide mention. The Westminster Dog Show devoted a twenty-minute segment to Shep which was aired on national television.

The community of Fort Benton later formed the Shep Committee to raise funds to build a lasting memorial for their famous and beloved dog. Etched bricks and miniature bronzes of Shep were sold to finance the project, which required $116,000 to complete. Renowned sculptor, Bob Scriver, created a heroic-sized bronze statue of Shep. The statue bears an amazing resemblance to Shep, capturing his stance with ears cocked, tail up, and his two front paws on part of a train rail, as he longingly gazes down at the track, waiting. To date, more than seven hundred memorial bricks have been placed around Shep's statue, many by people who have lost beloved pets.❧

Photo and artwork © George Rodrique

Tiffany   *Blue Dog*

Blue Dog
THE ETERNAL SPIRIT

Artist George Rodrique's "Blue Dog" paintings were inspired by his real-life dog, Tiffany. In his beautifully written and illustrated book Blue Dog, *Rodrique talked about the very special relationship he had with Tiffany, and how her love and spirit live on through his work.*

You know her as "Blue Dog," but when she first entered my life she went by the name "Tiffany," a black-and-white cross between a spaniel and a terrier. She filled my life with a rambunctious joy that made being sad around her almost impossible.

When it came to loving, Tiffany was totally uncritical. If I tried to throw out a pair of my old slippers, Tiffany would fetch them from the trash bin and secretly hide them at the back of the closet, where I kept her favorite blanket. The same for my old baseball caps, worn-out brushes, ripped T-shirts, and work gloves. And when I tried to take them away from her, she would lower her eyes, droop her head, and moan piteously. She would follow me out to the trash and look up at me as if imploring me not to drown her puppies. It wasn't worth it for me to show her who was boss. She beat me down, and I would always give in and let her have the slippers or the hat or the T-shirt. The minute I did, she would shiver with joy and drag those disgusting old things back to her closet, her tail wagging like a windshield wiper in a downpour.

When Tiffany was a puppy, she was such a whirling dervish that I had to bar her from my studio. I was always afraid that she'd get her paws in the oil paint or chew a canvas. But I lost that battle also, I couldn't stand her scratching at the door. I painted a picture of the two of us together, and propped it up right near her dog basket in the studio. The minute she saw it she seemed mesmerized, and from that time on, she would quietly sit in the studio, never making a sound or a sudden move until I would summon her for a scratch around the ears.

In the last days of her sickness, even as death approached, she was more concerned with loving me than begging for relief from suffering. One morning, I was painting in the studio. Tiffany was curled up in her basket, her head resting on her paws, her sad eyes looking at her favorite painting. My back was toward her, the slanted northern light gently warming me. I stopped my work, and unthinkingly snapped my fingers to bring her over for a scratch. But this time, she didn't come to me.

After Tiffany left me in 1980, I felt as though her spirit was trying to reach me through images she remembers, which developed into my paintings of "Blue Dog." She was there with me when my career began. She sat with me in my studio while I painted until all hours of the night. Although she was nothing special as a breed, she was a very special member of my family for twelve years ❧

—Excerpt from Blue Dog by George Rodrique with Lawrence Freundlich

Josh and campaign supporter, Megan Burell.

Josh

THE MUTT WHO WOULD BE PRESIDENT

According to the Federal Election Commission in Washington D.C., Josh was the first dog, (or mutt) to officially register as a candidate for U.S. President. In the summer of 1996, the canine candidate delivered a few barking speeches in front of the White House for admiring fans, after putting his paw print on an official "statement of candidacy."

Before running for president, the ambitious terrier mix had a successful career as an inspirational "speaker" for children nationwide. Dubbed "Josh the Wonder Dog" by his owner, Richard Stack, this incredible little dog certainly lived up to his name as his life story demonstrates.

In December 1983, Richard was watching a children's Christmas movie at his home in Maryland, and felt the movie was sending the

Photo ©Windmill Press

Richard Stack and Josh

wrong messages to kids about self-esteem. He decided to write a book that would teach kids to reach for high self-esteem, and chose a dog to be his main character. He began to write an inspirational story about a little mutt named Josh, who dreamed of being important.

Richard asked his uncle Charles, a commercial artist, to create the illustrations, and described to him how he imagined Josh should look. Although the final illustration was not exactly as Richard had envisioned, he was still quite pleased with it.

A few weeks later, Richard was out in his front yard getting the morning paper, when he suddenly stopped dead in his tracks. Standing right in front of him was a dog that looked identical to Charles's illustration of Josh. Sensing there was a special purpose for the dog ending up at his home, Richard took him in, and named him Josh after the character in his book. He finished the book about a year later, and named it *The Doggonest Christmas*.

In the summer of 1987, Richard left Josh with some friends while vacationing in Florida. While he was away, Josh was shot in the back by some gun-happy hoodlums in the neighborhood, and had to be rushed to the vet hospital for emergency surgery. Richard was devastated after hearing the terrible news and flew home immediately to be with Josh.

After a few days of recuperation at the hospital, Josh went home but was still in a lot of pain. It was difficult for him to walk, and the gunshot wound had left him with severe nerve damage, making it necessary for Richard to express Josh's bladder several times a day. After a few weeks of watching his friend in pain, Richard couldn't bear it any longer, and called to schedule euthanasia for Josh for the following day. The next morning, to Richard's amazement, Josh had a sudden and miraculous recovery. He seemed to be walking normally and didn't appear to be in any pain. The vet attributed Josh's amazing recovery to his strong will and determination.

Deeply moved by Josh's incredible will to live, Richard quit his full-time law practice to travel the country, and share Josh's inspirational story with children everywhere. Over the next nine years Josh and Richard visited more than eight hundred schools, and met thousands of children. As a result, Josh earned the coveted title of "The World's Most Petted Dog," in the 1997 *Guinness Book of World Records*, after being petted 408,127 times.

After Richard's first book was published in 1988, he wrote another book about the amazing story of Josh's life, titled *Josh the Wonder Dog*. During his fourteen years with Richard, Josh spread his inspirational message to thousands of children and adults across the country. His story was featured in several newspapers, and even made it to the *National Enquirer*.

In July 1997, at the age of fourteen, Josh died after a short bout with cancer. Although Richard knows there will never be another dog like Josh, he hopes to find another amazing mutt to continue his legacy❧

Josh's official Statement of Candidacy for U.S. President.

Courtesy of Green Hills Library, Palos Hills, Illinois

Felix

THE LEGENDARY FIREHOUSE MUTT

A boxer mix named Felix is touted as one of the most legendary fire-house dogs in history. In 1920, he was found as an injured stray outside a Chicago firehouse. Some caring firemen from Engine Co. 25 took him in and lovingly nursed him back to health. When no one claimed him, they happily adopted the dog as their official firehouse mascot. In years to follow, Felix returned the act of kindness by saving several lives, including those of the very same men who took him in.

Once while on a fire call, the men became trapped in a burning

building and were over-
come by smoke, and no
one could see through the
smoke to find them. Sud-
denly, Felix appeared at a
window and began barking
to alert fellow firefighters
to the whereabouts of his
trapped friends.

On another occasion
Felix saved a small infant
just moments away from

Courtesy of Green Hills Library, Palos Hills, Illinois

Felix taught himself to climb the fire ladder.

death in a burning building. Firefighters thought they had evacuated
everyone from the building, but Felix refused to leave, and stood by the
door barking persistently. A few of the men quickly ran back inside,
and were shocked to find a baby still in the building.

Felix was not only known for his heroic acts, but also for his intelligence. He quickly learned the fire-alert codes, and was always the first
one to leap on the fire truck when his friends were called to action. He
taught himself to climb up the fire ladder, and would get back down by
hopping on the back of a firefighter. Felix became a town hero, and was
loved by everyone. Children would often stop by the firehouse to bring
treats for him, and loud cheers could be heard whenever a fire truck
passed through town with Felix aboard.

When Felix passed away in 1926, the neighborhood mourned the
loss of their much beloved hero. A proper wake was held at the firehouse followed by an elaborate funeral ceremony, and local schools
were closed the day of his funeral. Felix was buried in a solid mahogany
casket donated by a local furniture store, and several children who
loved him served as pallbearers. Tears streamed down their faces as
they walked their friend to his final resting place.

More than sixty years after his death, Felix came back to life
through a Chicago librarian named Darlene Fillis. In 1986, a library

patron brought in a photo of Felix's wake, and a typed reminiscence from her mother, who had apparently first found the dog. Darlene was captivated by Felix's story, and wanted to know more. After learning that only a modest grave stone stood in his memory, she launched a fund-raising campaign to build a proper memorial.

Darlene and her daughter, April, ran off hundreds of flyers and news releases, calling for more information about Felix, and asking for donations to build a memorial statue. They received stories and photographs from several people who had known Felix when they were children, and others who knew some of the firefighters who worked with him.

For two years, Darlene and April devoted hundreds of hours to fund-raising efforts for Felix's memorial. After raising more than $10,000, a bronze statue bearing Felix's likeness was dedicated in a special ceremony near the Green Hills Library in Palos Hills, Illinois in July 1988.❖

Annie
THE RAILROAD DOG

During the Great Depression in the 1930s, it was all people could do to care for themselves, let alone their dogs. And certainly not a stray dog of unknown origin. But in the town of Fort Collins, Colorado, a bedraggled-looking collie mix caught the hearts of a few railway men from the Colorado and Southern Railroad.

The men found the dog shivering and starving outside the local blacksmith's shop, near the railway, and took pity on the frightened young pup. She was very timid at first, but after the rail workers came to visit her a few times, offering scraps of food, she began to warm up. She would gently take the food, and then lick their hands afterwards as a gesture of thanks.

They decided to take the dog back to the train depot, but first wanted to be sure she didn't belong to anyone. The blacksmith inside the shop where they had found her told them, "She's just a skinny mutt that

Courtesy of Arlene Ahlbrandt

Bronze statue of Annie.

nobody wants. I think she is a mixed-breed sheep dog. I'm going to get rid of her because she is going to have puppies." It was decided then and there that the men would adopt the dog as their official railway mascot.

They carried the dog in their arms and boarded the train to take her to her new home at the Fort Collins train depot. A special bed was made for her in the basement, and the railway workers promised each other that their little friend would never spend another night being alone, scared, and hungry. She now had a family and a place to call home.

They named their new mascot Annie, after a dog that Chris the brakeman had as a child. All of the men quickly grew to love Annie, and she loved them, but Chris was always her favorite. A few weeks after she came to live at the train depot, Annie's three puppies were born. Families who adopted the puppies were carefully selected by the railway workers to ensure that Annie's offspring would never have to endure what their mother had been through.

During a time of such dark despair, Annie brought a ray of sun-shine to the people of Fort Collins. She was always happy, with a tail that seemed to wag twenty-four hours a day. For the next fourteen years, she faithfully greeted passengers at the train depot.

Everyone who met Annie loved her. Newcomers were often amazed to see local people get off the train to run and greet Annie before greet-ing their families. It is said that many battle-weary, World War II sol-diers would sink to their knees, take Annie into their arms and cry for joy when they returned home by train.

When Annie was about twelve, Chris retired from the railway, but he still came to the station every day to take Annie for walks around town. The two would make daily visits to the local police and fire stations and then walk down the street to the Silver Grill Cafe, where Annie would happily dine on cooked scraps saved especially for her. Sometimes they would stop at the nearby meat market to collect bones the butcher had saved for Annie, and the ice cream shop where kids would run outside to greet Annie and offer her a few licks from their cones.

As Chris and Annie grew older together arthritis began to take its toll on the both of them. Their daily walks became shorter and slower. Sometimes they would just sit together on the porch at Chris's house, Annie laying quietly beside him, while he gently stroked her fur and talked to her.

At the age of fourteen, Annie passed away quietly in her sleep in her bed at the train depot. All who knew her were deeply saddened by her death especially her close friend Chris. The men of the Colorado and Southern Railroad broke all the rules and buried her right next to the tracks where she had spent her life. They erected a three-foot tall head-stone that reads: "From C and S Men to Annie. . . Our Dog."

It has been more than fifty years since Annie died, but she has never been forgotten. Today her grave site is a historical landmark, and has been surrounded by a wrought-iron fence with stone pillars, donated by the city of Fort Collins. For many years a mystery person has placed colorful artificial flowers on Annie's grave at different times during the year, and others who knew her when they were children often stop to visit her grave site. Annie is truly a cherished local legend.

A striking 29-inch bronze statue bearing Annie's likeness and friendly demeanor was created by Dawn Weimer, a local wildlife artist. In August 1998, the Fort Collins Public Library held a fund-raising dog walk event to purchase the statue, where it now has a permanent home.

Christopher (Chris the brakeman) Demuth's daughter, Loretta Burdette, collaborated with author Arlene Ahlbrandt on a charming children's book titled *Annie, the Railroad Dog.*

Courtesy of Arlene Ahlbrandt

Annie's grave site.

Sergeant Stubby

CHAPTER THREE

Mutts of War

*M*ore than thirty thousand dogs served in World War I and World War II as guards, protectors, confidants, and best friends to thousands of human soldiers. Although the majority of dogs trained for combat were purebred, some of the most memorable and heroic dogs of war were mutts who were often found as strays and adopted by soldiers as troop mascots.

◆ ◆ ◆

Stubby

THAT'S SERGEANT STUBBY

During World War I, in the summer of 1917, a homeless dog wandered into the training camp of the army's 102nd Infantry at Yale University. The young boxer-mix quickly endeared himself to the troops, particularly Private J. Robert Conroy, and was adopted as an unofficial member of the division. They named him Stubby, after his stub of a tail. Despite a "no pets allowed" policy, Stubby shared meals and sleeping quarters with the men and reportedly began mimicking their drills and marching exercises.

When it came time to go to war, Conroy and his colleagues smuggled the dog aboard a steamer headed for Europe. Stubby reached the trenches of the front line in February 1916, in the midst of a horrific battle. Although he had no formal training to cope with such nightmarish conditions, he calmly endured an unceasing barrage of shelling for the first thirty days. Stubby's caretakers were amazed by his cool under fire, and absolutely stunned when he voluntarily ventured out into the battle zone to seek out and comfort wounded soldiers still caught in the cross-fire. News of the dog's bravery and heroism reached the French village of Domremy, and after fighting subsided, the women of the town presented him with a hand-sewn chamois coat decorated with Allied flags and his name stitched in gold thread.

By war's end Stubby had been credited numerous times with saving his regiment from certain disaster. He would warn the men of incoming mortar shells by barking or hurling himself to the ground. One time he prevented the escape of a German spy by sinking his teeth into the seat of the man's pants refusing to let go. Whiffs of mustard gas, too faint to be detected by the human nose, sent Stubby into a barking tirade that warned soldiers to don protective gear. Stubby roused a sleeping soldier just in time to get both his and the soldier's masks on. The regiment had provided Stubby with his own makeshift gas mask, custom-fitted to accommodate his round head and flattened snout.

Stubby was also an experienced "therapy dog" long before animal visitations were proven to hasten the recovery time of the sick or seriously injured. He ministered to the troops in his own canine fashion, often cuddling up to wounded or shell-shocked soldiers, keeping them warm through a long winter's night. Sometimes he simply sat staring intently into the men's faces, his piercing hypnotic gaze calming and distracting them from their pain or grief. During a lull in the fighting at Toul, France, Stubby ventured out onto the battlefield and was wounded in the chest by a burst of enemy shrapnel. Yet during his own convalescence, Stubby took it upon himself to get out of his little bed and wander through the field hospital, visiting soldiers who, like him, were recovering from injuries received in the line of fire.

At one point Conroy was wounded and evacuated to a hospital in Paris. Hospital administrators granted an exception to their "no pets" rule and allowed Stubby to keep his friend Conroy company. Medics found Stubby's conduct impeccable, and the cathartic effect of his visits was noted by the physicians. On extended convalescence leave with Conroy in France, Stubby's fame continued to grow. He became the toast of Paris when he saved a little girl from being run over in the middle of a busy thoroughfare, and was frequently seen strolling about town wearing his chamois blanket, which now sported a rapidly growing array of honorary medals donated by friends and admirers.

Eighteen months after Stubby debarked on foreign soil, the war came to an end. He had served in at least eighteen major battles, and saw more action than most human soldiers. Back home he became a nationally acclaimed hero and eventually was received by Presidents Wilson, Harding, and Coolidge. General Pershing presented him with a gold medal and declared him a "hero of the highest caliber." After the war Stubby led more regimental parades than any dog in American history and was promoted to Honorary Sergeant, becoming the highest ranking dog to ever serve in the Army. He was also an honorary member of the Red Cross, the American Legion, and the YMCA, which issued him a membership card good for "three bones a day and a place to sleep."

Despite his nationwide fame, Stubby at times encountered prejudice against his kind—a mutt. In 1923, thousands of spectators hoping to see the little hero packed a national dog show in Boston. Breeders attempted to block his guest appearance, complaining that he was a mongrel and therefore had no business at an exhibition of pedigreed dogs. A show judge ruled against them, saying, "He may be a mutt, but he's done more than all of your dogs put together—Stubby stays!"❧

—Excerpted from MARY ELIZABETH THURSTON'S The Lost History of the Canine Race (Andrews & McMeel, 1996)

Photo courtesy of William T. Brown

Queenie
THE TWELVE-POUND WONDER

Sailors of subchaser 1302 who would never be caught showing tenderness towards each other, openly displayed their love for a small terrier mix named Queenie. While stationed in San Juan, Puerto Rico, a sailor from neighboring subchaser 1279 purchased Queenie from a small boy in exchange for a candy bar. His ship already had a canine mascot, so he asked a few of the sailors aboard 1302 if they could take Queenie. The men couldn't resist the adorable little dog, and after some fancy persuading, they talked their captain into taking her aboard as their mascot.

Queenie quickly captured the hearts of the entire crew and the captain. Lookouts on the bridge scanning the dark horizon for enemy subs gave Queenie their padded lookout chair to sleep on while they stood on the deck. If it rained, the men covered her with a raincoat. When the midnight watch received coffee and bologna sandwiches, Queenie happily ate her share along with the others on duty. And she was often found curled up in the lap of the sonar operator as the gear pinged and searched. Not a member of the crew, including the captain, could resist Queenie when she sat up to get attention—something she learned on her own.

One day while in Trinidad harbor, Queenie made a misstep and fell overboard. Gunners Mate, William T. Brown, who was fully clothed, immediately jumped in to save her. His shipmates later kidded him about the rescue, assuring him that Queenie could swim and that she never would have drowned.

In February 1946, subchaser 1302 sailed to Charleston Navy Yard for decommissioning. Some of the crew left for new assignments, and several sailors, including Brown, were discharged. But where would Queenie go? The subchaser was the only home she had ever known, and the crew was her only family. Everyone knew that Brown had been reared on a farm in south Alabama where his parents still lived, and voted for him to take Queenie home to his parents' farm.

Brown built a special traveling box for Queenie with places for food and water, and hand-lettered her name on the top. The captain wrote an honorable discharge for Queenie, making her an official veteran of World War II. Queenie's captain and fellow crew members bid her a sad farewell. She would always sit up like a person at any excuse, and as she pulled away from the ship for the last time, she sat up on the dinghy seat with all of the importance of an admiral.

Brown's parents were eager to meet Queenie since she'd been the subject of nearly every letter he'd written them for the past two years. It took Queenie several days to make the switch from sea life to farm life, but she soon settled in and began to enjoy her new life as a farm dog. Brown's parents became very fond of Queenie, and she of them. She lived eight more years on the farm until her death in August 1952.

Brown still reminisces about the times he shared with his little ship-mate. He speaks proudly of her accomplishments, and of how special she was to him and his fellow crew members. "Queenie drew our subchaser crew together into a close-knit family as no human could have done. The value of having that little dog to love, care for, and talk to during long, boring antisubmarine cruises was incalculable. To this day she stands out as the most memorable shipmate of my six years at sea❧"

Chips
THE MUTT WITH A PURPLE HEART

One of the most famous of all war dogs was a shepherd mix named Chips. He was a feisty dog with a mind of his own, but it was Chips's stubborn personality that ended up saving the lives of his human com-rades in a surprise attack in Italy during World War II. Chips earned a Silver Star and a Purple Heart for his daring heroics, making him the most highly decorated war dog in history.

Shortly after Chips and his comrades made their way to the shores of Sicily, they spotted what they thought was an abandoned pillbox where they could take a short rest. Against his handler's orders, Chips took off running directly into the pillbox where six Italian soldiers were waiting with machine guns. A round of fire was heard, then there was dead silence.

The American soldiers couldn't see or hear Chips, and were sure he had been killed. When the men made their way to the pillbox, they were astounded to find Chips very alive and holding onto the throat of the enemy gunman with his teeth. Five other Italian soldiers were standing there terrified with their arms raised in surrender.

The men that Chips had saved wanted to honor their friend. The lieutenant in command recommended Chips for the Silver Star and Purple Heart for his "courageous action in single-handedly eliminating a dangerous machine gun nest, and causing the surrender of its crew."

Courtesy of American Kennel Club Dog Museum

Chips

Chips was presented with the medals, but unfortunately his honor was short lived. The Army's top brass stated that the Silver Star and Purple Heart were only given to men, not dogs, and poor Chips was stripped of his medals.

The soldiers were quite upset that Chips's medals were revoked, and decided to take matters into their own hands. They presented him with a special theater ribbon adorned with an arrowhead signifying the assault landing at Sicily, and a battle star for each of the eight battles in which Chips served.

After the war, Chips went home to live in Pleasantville, New York where he seemed to adapt easily to civilian life. Unfortunately, he died only seven months later due to complications from war injuries.❧

©Collection of Mary E. Thurston

Boots

THE BOB HOPE OF WAR DOGS

Boots was sort of like a canine version of Bob Hope during World War II. He entertained thousands of troops at USO shows with his comedy act and tricks and was credited with selling $9 million worth of war bonds through fund-raising events. But Boots was really a Hollywood dog, and his story is truly a rags to riches tale.

Professional animal trainer, Bert Rose, "discovered" Boots when he was just a newborn pup. He was the runt of the litter and was refusing to eat. Rose's friends thought they should put the poor little dog out of its misery, but Rose knew better. He sensed something very special about the sickly pup and offered to take him in. Rose nurtured and cared for

Boots, and the dog responded with great affection and devotion.

Rose soon realized that Boots had real "star qualities" and began teaching the dog a long list of commands in order to prep him for Hollywood. Eventually Boots learned an eight hundred word vocabulary, which is about one-third of the average human's vocabulary. Movie studios were quite impressed with Boots's talents, and quickly signed him on as a canine actor. He went on to star in more than a dozen films and won an Oscar for his performance in the Paramount movie *Emergency Squad*. At the height of his career Boots earned $3,000 a week, quite an impressive salary for a canine star in the 1940s.

An actor who once watched Boots at work on a movie set described the dog's uncanny ability to follow a long succession of commands. "When the set-up for this first scene was ready, Rose called to the dog and said, 'Now listen Boots, in this scene you jump through that window, walk slowly over to the desk, open the drawer, take out the knife and carry it to that man over there. Now I'll repeat that, and afterwards, when you hear me say "action" we'll go through it for rehearsal.' That, and that alone sufficed. Boots did exactly as he was told, word for word." Boots performed a sequence of commands similar to this for troops at more than 150 army camps during the war, and gave a command performance for President Franklin D. Roosevelt in Georgia.

Boots died at age sixteen, and was laid to rest at the famous Hartsdale Pet Cemetery in New York. He was buried with a proper funeral ceremony attended by a host of Hollywood friends and fans. When news of his death reached the press, obituaries appeared in newspapers throughout the country❧

Sinbad
SAILOR FIRST CLASS

More than two-thousand dogs saw action serving in the U.S. Coast Guard during World War II. The vast majority, consisting of larger breeds, were employed on beach patrols, while other smaller breeds earned their keep as mascots on board Coast Guard ships. The most famous of war sea dogs was a rottweiler and beagle mix named Sinbad. He was the veteran mascot of the U.S. Coast Guard cutter *Campbell.*

Sinbad was smuggled aboard the *Campbell* by one of the crew in the winter of 1937, while the ship was docked overnight in New York. Uncertain as to how the captain would react, the crew kept the dog out of sight until the ship was safely out of the harbor. Once at sea, Sinbad's playful antics made him a favorite among all hands, including the captain. And before the patrol was ended, Sinbad was sworn in as "Seaman Pooch," complete with his own service jacket and health record.

If there ever was a dog born to go to sea, it was Sinbad. He could hold his own on a pitching deck as well as any other member of the crew. He could scurry up and down ladders, loved to swim, and like a true sailor, loved his coffee, hot and black.

During his eleven-year reign as the ship's chief morale booster and good luck charm, Sinbad earned the admiration and affection of his shipmates; national fame for his shipboard exploits; and a few harsh words from U.S. government officials for the embarrassment that he caused them by his uninhibited shenanigans while ashore on foreign lands.

His shipmates, unsure of his ancestry, were prone to say that Sinbad had all the earmarks of a "Curbstone Setter," with a touch of "Sooner Hound" thrown in. Whatever his heritage, along the way he developed quite a sweet tooth, which drove him to the canteen each time that sundry emporium was declared "Open." He refused to budge until someone bought him a candy bar.

Sinbad enjoyed lapping up a cold beer—a habit he picked up early in his career, while the *Campbell* was berthed at Staten Island. His usual

Campbell *Commander, Gilbert I. Lynch, shakes hands with Sinbad at his retirement ceremony in 1948.*

routine was to dash across the tracks to the local bistro, well in advance of his crew mates. Once inside, the friendly bartender would draw him a saucer of beer, which would be paid for by the first *Campbell* sailor to enter the place. In later years, Sinbad was said to have a change purse attached to his collar so that he could pay his own way.

Sinbad's main job aboard ship was keeping up the crew's morale. He loved everyone on the *Campbell*, but never really attached himself to anyone in particular. He was at his best in a crowd, and cheerfully played with any sailor who was interested. His favorite toy was a simple metal washer, which he rolled back and forth across deck. Whenever he saw a crew member looking lonely or depressed, the washer would appear and Sinbad would go into his routine. His amusing antics were usually enough to restore the spirits of even the most down-hearted sailor.

Sinbad was on board the *Campbell* through good times and bad during his long career. The ship was assigned to protect convoys as they crossed the North Atlantic carrying men and supplies for the European war. On one occasion, the *Campbell* was making a return trip from Europe with the convoy, when one of the freighters was hit by a German sub. The *Campbell* turned back to help the crewmen on the disabled ship, and halfway through the rescue operation an explosion was heard. A German sub shot a torpedo at the *Campbell*, but it exploded before reaching the ship.

The *Campbell* retaliated, attacking six submarines that night, and ramming another, sinking it to the bottom. Throughout the ordeal, Sinbad growled and barked defiantly at the enemy submarines. He knew it was a life and death situation, and wanted to do what he could to help his fellow crewmen.

The account of the *Campbell*'s victory over the enemy sub made headlines and Sinbad received his share of the acclaim. Later, when the *Campbell* was brought back to Charleston, North Carolina for an overhaul, Sinbad was sent by train to New York to receive a proper hero's welcome. He went to City Hall for the welcoming ceremonies, then rode in a Jeep parade to the District Office on Broadway, where he held a press conference and posed for pictures. He then set off on an eighteen thousand mile tour with the Coast Guard Recruiting Team, making guest appearances on more than one hundred radio shows.

When he later returned to his home on the *Campbell*, Sinbad had a short romance with another mascot on the nearby cutter *Winnebago*. An official message from *Campbell* to Headquarters, read: "Sinbad father of twins. Mother, son and daughter doing nicely. Sinbad has passed cigars to all hands."

After spending more than eleven years aboard the *Campbell*, Sinbad was transferred to the Barnegat Lifeboat Station in September 1948. He enjoyed semi-retirement there for three more years until he died at the age of sixteen in December 1951. He was laid to rest beneath the station flagpole.❖

Photo courtesy of Atwater Kent Museum

Philly, preserved by her fellow comrades.

Philly
FRONT LINE BATTLE MUTT

During World War I, a young soldier training at Camp Meade, Maryland, found a stray puppy and smuggled her into the barracks of Company A of the 315th Infantry. Other soldiers in the barracks quickly fell in love with the spaniel mix and voted to adopt her as their official mascot. The majority of enlistees in the 79th Division were from Philadelphia, earning the unit the official designation of "Philadelphia's Own," hence the name Philly for their little mascot.

When the 315th was ordered to France, one of the men tucked Philly into his coat sleeve and smuggled her aboard the troop ship. In the months that followed, she saw active service at Montfaucon, Nantillois, and in the deadly hills of La Grande Montagne above Verdun. She was wounded, gassed, hospitalized, and even received a couple of improvised Purple Hearts from her admiring troops. She was so good at guard duty—barking to alert soldiers of sneak attacks—that a German commander placed a bounty of 50 deutsche marks on her head.

Philly had a real service record, made out just like that of any other soldier. She proudly wore a custom-made blue army coat, adorned with symbols for service and bravery. A wound chevron, for the time she got shrapnel in her tail during battle; a six months' overseas service stripe; a corporal's chevron; and the blue-gray shield of the 79th Division.

After the war, Philly returned to the United States. She paraded with the 315th in Washington, D.C., and though her marching was strictly against Army regulations, President Woodrow Wilson was delighted by her presence. Over the next twelve years, Philly lived with Sgt. Charles "Butch" Hermann, in Frankford, Pennsylvania. She attended all of the 315th Infantry reunions, where she dined on her favorite dish of liver and cake, and the men did "war dances" around her.

Weakened by old age, Philly died at the age of fifteen. Hermann had always planned to have her mounted when she died, but when the end came, he was without a job in the midst of the Depression and couldn't afford a taxidermist's fees. So, in the dead of night, when his neighbors were asleep, he buried Philly as close by as possible—under his driveway.

Norris S. Barratt, Jr., Captain of Company A, under whom Philly had served overseas, felt this was not a fitting end for the little mascot loved by so many. So, again in the dead of night, he had her dug up from under Hermann's driveway. He then took up a collection among the 7,500 men of the 315th to pay for a taxidermist. Philly was later mounted and given a place of honor at the battalion's headquarters on Wissahickon Avenue.

When the 315th ended in 1995, Philly was presented to the Atwater Kent Museum in Philadelphia where she now stands inside a glass case surrounded by other 315th memorabilia including helmets, bullets, gas masks, and dog tags✥

Fido

— CHAPTER FOUR —

Presidential Mutts

*D*uring the terms of forty-two U.S. Presidents, 190 children, and about four hundred animals have been a part of the "First Families." Nearly all the presidents had some kind of animal companion. Although dogs and cats were the most common, a hippo, a bear, an antelope, and a snake are among some of the more unusual animal companions of past presidents. Goats, chickens, sheep, fish, ponies, and rabbits have also resided at the White House.

According to Dr. Ronnie G. Elmore, associate dean of the College of Veterinary Medicine at Kansas State University and a self-appointed archivist of the presidential pet gallery, George Washington had thirty-six dogs, which he bred to create the foxhound breed.

During Bill Clinton's presidency, a nationwide "Adopt-a-Mutt" campaign was launched by several humane organizations after Clinton bid $3,500 to purchase a golden retriever at a charity auction. The White House was flooded with thousands of letters encouraging Clinton to adopt a shelter dog and send a humane message to the American public. But to no avail. In 1998, Clinton received a chocolate lab named Buddy as a gift.

Only five presidents to date have embraced mutts as "First Dogs." Here are their stories.

◆ ◆ ◆

Fido

ABRAHAM LINCOLN

President Lincoln was known for his kindness to animals, especially dogs. As a youngster, he rescued a mutt that he found in the woods with a broken leg. He made a splint for the injured dog and took it to a nearby cave where he made a makeshift bed out of leaves and dirt. He named the dog Honey after her yellowish coloring. Every day Lincoln visited her and brought her food and water. When Honey was well enough, Lincoln brought her home to live. A short time later when Lincoln became trapped in a cave, it was Honey who led the rescue party to find him.

When Lincoln was inaugurated in 1861, he opted not to take his much beloved dog Fido with him to the White House. The dog was easily scared by crowds of people and loud noises, and Lincoln felt it would be best to leave him behind. The Roll family, who were close friends of the Lincolns, agreed to take Fido in and care for him. Lincoln gave specific orders that the dog should never be tied up, should never be scolded for entering the house with dirty paws, and must always be allowed in the dining room during mealtimes to dine on table scraps.

During his presidency, Lincoln had other dogs in the White House, but none who were as special to him as Fido. He checked in often with the Roll family for updates on Fido, and on many occasions would send small gifts of dog biscuits or bones to his friend.

Lincoln was assassinated on April 14, 1865. His body was taken back to Springfield for burial where Fido still lived. The dog looked noticeably forlorn as he watched the funeral procession that was followed by Old Bob, Lincoln's horse and Fido's good pal. Less than a year later, Fido met with a tragic end himself. One day he had wandered from the Rolls's home, and was fatally stabbed by a drunk who mistook the dog's playful gestures for aggressiveness ❧

Theodore Roosevelt Collection, Harvard College Library

Skip sitting in his favorite spot, on President Roosevelt's lap.

Skip

THEODORE ROOSEVELT

The Roosevelt family had nothing short of a zoo during their years in the White House. Numerous dogs, cats, and even a pony were among the four-legged residents. A mutt named Tip was First Lady Edith Roosevelt's favorite dog. But she made it perfectly clear that any servant who degraded Tip by calling him a mutt would be fired on the spot. When Tip ran away, Edith replaced him with another dog from the pound, which she named Mutt in order to eliminate any future name-calling.

President Roosevelt's favorite dog was a small brownish mutt named Skip. It was a rare occasion that the President was seen without Skip in tow. The little dog followed him everywhere, even joining him in the saddle for frequent horseback rides. Whenever the President sat down for a meeting or a rest, Skip would jump on his lap for a short snooze.

Skip was also a favorite of the Roosevelt children, especially seven-year old Archie who loved to run relay races with him. As Roosevelt wrote in his journal, "Archie would spread his legs, bend over and hold Skip between them, then he would shout 'on your mark Skip, ready, go,' and would shove Skip back while he ran as fast as he possibly could to the other end of the hall, while Skip scrambled wildly with his paws on the smooth floor."

When the children were done playing for the night, Skip would go find the President, and jump into his lap for a snooze while the President did his nightly reading. And when it was time to retire for the evening, Skip hopped onto the bed in his designated spot right beneath the President's feet.

Skip enjoyed playing with Archie and the other children, but his favorite playmate was Archie's pony, Algonquin. The two would often play chase on the White House lawn, and when they both became a bit tired, Algonquin would stand still and let Skip hop on his back for a short ride.

Skip died during Roosevelt's last year in office in 1907. The President was grief stricken when his friend died, but found some solace in the fact that, as he stated, "He had a happy little life❖"

Yuki

LYNDON B. JOHNSON

Yuki was not the only dog Lyndon Johnson had during his presidency, but was certainly his most favorite. The "first mutt" had free run of the White House, and could often be found sitting on the President's lap while he conducted business in the Oval Office. The pair were insepa-rable and they even sang duets together. The President would whistle a tune and Yuki would throw his head back and howl in unison.

Before taking up residency at the White House, Yuki was found as

Photo © Yoichi R. Okamoto, LBJ Library Collection

Yuki and President Johnson sing a duet for a visitor at the White House.

a stray at a Texas gas station by Johnson's daughter Luci. When Luci later married, Yuki attended the wedding dressed in a special red velvet outfit for the occasion. When it came time for family wedding portraits, the President and Lady Bird got into quite an argument because he insisted that Yuki be included in the pictures. She absolutely refused and demanded that Yuki leave the room. Lady Bird got her way, but afterwards she and her husband were not on speaking terms for days.

Johnson was notorious for his flatulence and would often blame the offensive odor on poor Yuki. Everyone always knew who the source was, but they would act like they really believed it was Yuki to avoid embarrassing the President. Some people began referring to Yuki as "the four-legged secret service agent," since one of her main duties was protecting the President from his embarrassing habit.

When Yuki fell suddenly ill and had to be rushed to a nearby animal hospital, the distressed President exclaimed, "Yuki means more to me than anything in the White House!" Yuki made a full recovery, but Lady Bird was very annoyed with her husband for making that statement.

After Johnson's presidency, Yuki retired with him to his Texas ranch and was by Johnson's side when he died of a heart attack in 1973 ❧

Courtesy of John F. Kennedy Library

Pushinka

JOHN F. KENNEDY

In 1962, Premier Nikita Khrushchev sent a white spaniel mix named Pushinka as a gift to Caroline Kennedy. The gesture was made in an effort to reduce tensions with the United States following the Cuban missile crisis. Pushinka (which means "fluffy" in Russian) was the daughter of Streika, the first Russian orbiting space-dog and Pushok, a Russian canine hero. The Kennedys were very happy to accept the dog, but before Pushinka was allowed into the White House, she was thoroughly searched by the CIA for possible microphone bugs hidden in her fur.

Pushinka and the Kennedy's Welsh terrier Charlie instantly hit it off, and the two soon had a litter of four pups, which JFK referred to as "Pupniks." Two of the pups were already spoken for, and a letter writing contest for children was used to find homes for the other two. More than ten thousand letters flooded the White House. One of the best letters could not be declared a winner because the sender forgot to include his or her name and address. The letter read: "I will raise the puppy to be a true Democrat and to bite all Republicans☙"

Grits

JIMMY CARTER

Grits and Amy Carter

When the Carter family first moved into the White House, their only pet was a cat named Missy. President Carter's daughter, Amy, was eager to have a dog as part of the first family, so when her school teacher offered her a small black-and-white puppy, she happily accepted. Amy named her new dog Grits. During her first year in the White House, Amy played host with Grits to visiting canine celebrities including Benji, and Sandy, the dog from the Broadway musical, "Annie."

Amy grew very attached to Grits, but unfortunately her parents didn't share the same sentiment. The President became increasingly annoyed with the dog's stubborn personality, especially when it came to housebreaking. Poor Grits just couldn't seem to get the hang of it and left stains on the carpeting in several White House rooms. Upon orders from her father, Amy reluctantly returned Grits back to her teacher☙

Keller

— CHAPTER FIVE —

Amazing Mutts

*A*ll of the dogs in this chapter are truly amazing and remarkable in different ways. When I was faced with the difficult task of deciding which dog should lead this chapter, it had to be Keller, paws down. Her story left an unforgettable impression in my mind and heart.

Pets with handicaps or disabilities don't stand much of a chance for being adopted. They are often regarded as "unadoptable" and are sometimes euthanized before they have the chance they so deserve for a loving home. Depending on the severity of the illness, or handicap, a "special needs" pet can involve a lot of work. But as the following two stories demonstrate, caring for these special animals is repaid many times over with tremendous love and affection.

◆ ◆ ◆

Keller

SEEING WITH THE HEART

At only three months old she was discarded by her owner, and deemed "absolutely unadoptable" by an animal shelter clerk. Surely no one would want a small black-and-tan chihuahua mix with bat-like ears, who was born with no eyes, and therefore completely blind. But the shelter's staff veterinarian saw beyond the dog's handicap, noticing her charming personality and pulled her off the list of animals awaiting euthanasia.

Animal Trustees of Austin, an organization that helps find homes for pets with "special needs," welcomed the little dog with open arms. Her charm instantly captured the hearts of the group's founding members, Missy McCullough and Bobbie Caviness, who christened her "Keller," after Helen Keller.

Missy and Bobbie were astounded by Keller's quick adaptation to their home. In less than a few weeks she had made a mental "blueprint" of their house in order to steer clear of furniture and closed doors, and had memorized the entire layout of the three-level home. She now runs at a full gallop from room to room, rarely hitting an obstacle.

Keller became so confident in her abilities that she once deliberately leapt off a fifteen-foot indoor balcony, landing on the sofa below. Missy recalled the startling incident. "Keller crouched down, then leaped clear of the railing, paws outstretched like Superman. Incredibly she remembered where the couch was below, and landed square on the pillows. I think she just wanted to know what it was like to fly."

Twice a year Missy and Bobby travel with Keller and their four other dogs to a vacation home in Colorado. Although Keller has not been there for six months at a time, she'll walk in the door, and immediately remember her way around. "Once she's been somewhere it's like she has the ability to computerize in her head a schematic drawing of where she is," explained Missy. "All the senses that she uses: taste, smell, texture, temperature, and sounds, are programmed into her little computer for when she returns back to that same place again. She never forgets—it's the most incredible thing to observe."

Keller has become the mother hen to other foster dogs living at Missy and Bobbie's home. Young puppies traumatized by early separations from their mothers find a sympathetic playmate in Keller. And adult dogs many times her size follow her lead as she teaches them to bark at strange noises or ask for treats.

A toy fox terrier named Norman was a fear biter who attacked everyone, including fellow dogs. He would not allow any dogs to get close to him, except for Keller. It was as if he sensed that she was there to help him. Thanks to Keller, Norman learned to control his biting impulse, to play gently with puppies, and to seek out and accept human affection. After a few months Norman was sleeping with Keller in her tee-pee style bed, with one tiny arm flung across her shoulder.

Keller poses with the "Keller Doll."

Keller has become quite a celebrity in Austin, Texas. As the organization's proud mascot, she has led numerous demonstrations, and was instrumental in convincing the city animal shelter to replace its broken-down carbon-monoxide euthanasia chambers with humane lethal injection. She has appeared numerous times on the local news, and a stuffed animal bearing her likeness, named the "Keller Doll," was sold as a fund-raising item for Animal Trustees.

Missy and Bobby believe that many people could learn a lesson from Keller. "This little dog rejects no one. In the process, she gives people, and animals like Norman, a much-needed dose of unconditional love. Keller sees beauty in everybody—not with her eyes, but with her heart❖"

Tom Gorman

Runway and Becky Gorman

Runway
CAN'T KEEP A GOOD MUTT DOWN
–Becky Gorman

There is so much involved in the fight that we've gone through to keep our beloved Runway with us. The fight began when he was only six weeks old. In 1991, my husband Tom and I decided to adopt a dog. We visited several shelters searching for that one special dog. As soon as we spotted this little black puff ball, later named Runway, we fell instantly in love.

The shelter was planning to euthanize him, along with his mother and other litter mates. Tom had to plead with them for Runway's life. Because Runway was only six weeks old, they said he was too young to be adopted. They were putting his mother to sleep, so he would have no way to nurse. "We'll be his mother, we'll take the best care of him, I promise you," Tom pleaded. Luckily the shelter gave in. Our first battle for Runway was won, and we took him home that day.

Runway was unique from the first moment we got him. He had a mind of his own, but was very devoted to us from the start. His heritage was just as unique as his personality. Part Chesapeake Bay retriever, part shepherd, part chow, and part pit bull. Now how's that for a *real* Heinz 57!

When we adopted Runway, we made a commitment to love and protect him forever. In the seven years that we've had him, that love has been challenged several times. In one situation we ending up selling our ocean-front condominium because Runway had grown over the "weight limit" for pets, and the association refused to let us keep him. This situation was followed by Runway blowing out his right knee, which required a surgical specialist to repair it.

Our greatest challenge with Runway came in 1997, while we were living in a beautiful log cabin up on a mountain in Pegram, Tennessee. Runway loved the new surroundings and all of the different smells and sounds of nature. On Memorial Day, he must have caught the scent of a deer or something and took off running. When we found him a short time later, he had been struck by a car. Runway always wears a red bandanna with his initials on it (RG for Runway Gorman). His bandanna had come off when he was hit, and it was lying on the shoulder of the road. If it wasn't for that bandanna coming off, we may have never found him. Whoever hit him didn't have the decency to stop and help him, or to contact us.

We rushed Runway to an emergency veterinary clinic in town. We knew it was probably serious by the look on the doctor's face when he tried pressing on Runway's toes on his hind legs. He didn't move, or even realize that the doctor was touching him.

The doctor was about 95 percent sure that Runway's spinal cord had been severed and felt that putting him to sleep would be the best thing to do. We just couldn't make a decision until we knew about the other 5 percent. Fortunately the vet had an MRI machine on site, and they performed a scan on Runway. Three agonizing days later we got the results back. By the grace of God, that other 5 percent came through for us. Runway's spinal cord was not completely severed, but

Tom Gorman

Runway still enjoys swimming with the help of a boat bumper attached to his cart.

he would still never be able to use his hind legs again.

The doctor knew we wanted to keep Runway alive, as long as he wasn't suffering. He talked to us about getting a special wheelchair-like device for animals called the K9 Cart. He explained that it would be a big responsibility to have a dog in a K9 Cart and there's always a chance that the dog won't adjust to it. We opted to give the cart a try and fortunately Runway adapted to it quite well.

It has been a little more than a year since Runway's biggest battle. But this is one he surely won. He goes about his business just as he did before—running, fetching, giving kisses, and believe it or not, even swimming. The swimming wasn't the easiest to master though. We tried doggie lifejackets, tires, and everything imaginable to help him stay afloat. Then one day, a friend suggested using a small boat bumper, and we attached to the back of his cart, and off he went.

Runway goes everywhere with us, and does just about everything he did before the accident. Even when he's not in his cart, he can still run and fetch by using his two front legs and dragging his hind legs along the ground. If he wants to play ball, he'll drag himself to get the ball, then drop it in front of you. When he hears the wrapper on the cheese, he'll come running. We have to put him in and out of his cart, but he can maneuver around quite well. If he gets caught on something, he'll backup and then move to the left or right to free himself. Sometimes when he's going too fast and makes a quick turn, the cart will flip over. But that's okay, we're always nearby to flip him upright again. And he can't scratch behind his ears or neck anymore, but that's okay too, because we can do that for him.

The only thing that's really different now, is we have to help Runway express his bladder four times a day, and move his bowels, since he's unable to do it on his own. Having to work around his schedule does impede with what we're doing sometimes, but we always find a way to work it out—Runway comes first. Our friends are all very understanding, and are gracious enough to work things around Runway's schedule when we make plans together.

Seeing Runway's amazing ability to endure great difficulties and still have a positive outlook on life has been a real inspiration to us. In fact, we are planning to introduce him to the school boards in our area to suggest using him as a teaching tool. We would like Runway to teach younger children about the importance of looking both ways before crossing the street, and to teach older children and even adults to feel more comfortable relating to people who are handicapped. We hope to teach people that what Runway wants is the same as any human being in a similar situation—to be treated as a person and not a disease. They need to be touched and spoken to the same way Runway does. That is the reason Runway knows he is okay—because we treat him like the same dog he was before. He is still our wonderful mutt whom we love more than anything❧

Duque

$15,000 MUTT FOR A DAY

–Glen Peltz

In the summer of 1998, a somewhat distraught woman ran into our jewelry shop in Laguna Beach, California. "It's my puppy," she said frantically," can I leave him here with you, just for a half an hour?" Just then a small black ball of fur with large pointed ears, poked its nose out from under the towel in the basket the woman was holding. My father reluctantly agreed to watch the pup. A half an hour later, he received a phone call from the woman. "I can't keep the dog, could you please take it to the pound for me?" Without giving it another thought, he quickly replied, "Not a chance, I'm keeping him!"

We named our new friend Duque, after his part-poodle heritage, the other part chow. From that day on, Duque became the official store greeter, ready with a big wag of the tail to anyone who would offer him a belly rub. He seemed very unimpressed by all of the sparkling jewels our customers brought in for cleaning, but he became quite interested in the jewelry steam cleaner. Each time my father or I used the machine, Duque would jump up and try to catch the burst of steam in his mouth as it came out of the nozzle. As soon as he heard the machine start up, he came running.

Word of Duque's amusing antics began to spread. A TV show called "Prime Time Pets" called to ask us if Duque could perform this crazy trick in front of the camera and we gladly consented. Within weeks of the show's airing, Duque became a canine celebrity. Dozens of people began stopping by our shop just to catch a glimpse of Duque jumping up to bite at the steam bursts.

His real claim to fame however, occurred about a month later. In the summer of 1993, a regular client stopped by the shop to have her diamond ring cleaned. My father held the ring in a tweezer-like device under the nozzle of the machine and turned it on. As always, Duque was right there, his tail wagging excitedly as he jumped up to catch the burst of steam. Suddenly my father looked down and the ring was gone. "The dog swallowed the ring," he said jokingly, thinking that it had just been knocked to the floor. But after a fruitless search, it was concluded that Duque really did swallow the woman's $15,000 ring, diamonds and all!

The customer was in no mood to let nature take its course, and demanded that Duque be operated on immediately to retrieve her ring. Fortunately my father was able to convince the woman to wait until he took Duque in for X-rays to be absolutely sure the ring was there. X-rays confirmed that indeed Duque had quite an expensive appetite. The veterinarian administered a potion which immediately caused Duque to bring up the goods, and the ring was retrieved in perfect condition.

The following week, Duque's photo and incredible story were featured on the second page of the *National Enquirer*, the *Los Angeles Times*, and several other newspapers. He even got a joke from Jay Leno, and was "interviewed" on radio shows across the country.

Duque was the most valuable mutt in town for a day, but to our family he will always be the "gem of our hearts❀"

Photo © L.J. Peters Photography

Charlie and Helen Thayer

Charlie
THE ARCTIC EXPLORER

At the age of sixty-one, Helen Thayer has fulfilled many of her lifelong dreams of adventure. At fifty-six, she kayaked and walked 1,200 miles through the Amazon. And a few years ago she recently finished walking 1,400 miles across the Sahara Desert. But one of Helen's most amazing and memorable adventures to date was her solo trek to the magnetic North Pole in 1988, at the age of fifty.

After many years of mountaineering, including climbing the highest peaks in North and South America and the Soviet Union, Helen decided the time had come for a new challenge. After two years of preparation and planning, she set out to become the first woman to travel by ski and foot alone to the North Pole.

Three days before her departure, she made a last-minute decision to adopt a black husky and Newfoundland mix to accompany her on the expedition. She purchased the dog from an Inuit who used him and other sled dogs as tools and not as pets. Like most sled dogs, this dog had no name, was fed frozen seal meat twice a week, and chewed ice for water.

Helen named her dog Charlie and together they set off on a grueling 27-day, 365-mile journey to the magnetic North Pole. They faced fierce wind and weather, with wind chill temperatures dropping to one hundred degrees below zero. They trekked across breaking sea ice that tilted under their feet, and howling arctic storms that blew their food and equipment into oblivion. At one point, Helen's eyelids froze shut, and one eye was seriously injured.

The brave duo lived through many exciting adventures as well as frightening encounters with polar bears. Charlie had been specially trained to alert humans to polar bears and saved Helen's life many times during their trip. She credits much of her survival and perseverance to the intimate relationship between her and Charlie. When they were just seven days away from reaching the North Pole, a storm destroyed Helen's food supply and fuel for melting ice to drink. Although she was starving, she refused to take any of Charlie's remaining dog food for herself. On April 27, 1988, Helen and Charlie finally reached their destination, making them the first solo dog and woman team to ever reach the North Pole.

At journey's end, Charlie returned with Helen to her home in Snohomish, Washington. There he was introduced to a brand new world of grass, trees, flowers, and rain, in addition to Helen's three other dogs, five goats, two donkeys, and one cat. Not only did the once nameless dog now have a name, but he had a loving family and home for the first time in his life. Helen chronicled her amazing adventure with Charlie in the best-selling book *Polar Dream*.

With sled dog days far behind him, Charlie enjoys daily ten-mile jogs with Helen and her husband Bill, and also accompanies them on mountain climbs, hikes, and ski trips. Charlie is between twelve and fourteen years old, but as Helen says, "He's as fit as a six or seven year old dog." She prepares daily home-cooked meals for Charlie and her

Helen Thayer

Charlie and Helen on their trek to the magnetic North Pole.

other dogs and takes Charlie once a month to the chiropractor and acupuncturist. Together with Helen, Charlie makes regular visits to local schools where he circulates through the crowd offering kisses and a wagging tail.

For her sixtieth birthday Helen set out on a solo trek to the South Pole. Two hundred miles and twenty-one days into her journey, she injured her leg in a freak accident with her sled. She had pinched a nerve, badly bruised herself, and fell headfirst into the ice. That night, she activated an emergency beacon, and was later rescued. Dogs aren't allowed near the South Pole because there is a false belief that they can transmit disease to seals, so Helen was unable to take Charlie and desperately missed him on her journey. She brought a stuffed dog along to remind her of Charlie and to help her through the never-ending days and lonely nights.❖

To read about Helen's other incredible adventures, Internet users can log onto: www.goals.com

Barbara Herman

Dennis Walters and Muffin

Muffin, Mulligan, Hogan
THREE MUTTS MAKE A "HOLE-IN-ONE"

Hogan is a talented mathematician, able to add and subtract by barking accordingly; Mulligan was able to tee-up a golf ball, wave, and give a hi-five; and Muffin just slept a lot, but she had an irresistible personality and was as cute as they come. Three amazing mutts, each in his or own way, but what is equally amazing is the remarkable story of their best friend and companion, Dennis Walters.

At twenty four, Dennis was well on his way to a pro golf career—a dream he had since childhood. In July 1974, while driving a three-wheel golf cart down a slope on a New Jersey course, the brakes failed causing the cart to lose control and flip over. Dennis was thrown to the ground and knocked unconscious. When he came to he could feel nothing in his legs. He was permanently paralyzed. He spent the next six months in the hospital, and doctors told him that he'd never be able to play golf again.

The accident was physically and emotionally devastating for Dennis. And although his family and friends were constantly by his side to offer their love and support, he still felt somehow alone. He recalled cherished memories of dogs (all adopted mutts) he had as a child—memories of the special love and companionship he shared with each of them, and decided this would be a good time to bring a new dog into his life.

After searching for several weeks, he found a dog he wanted to adopt at a local shelter. When he went up to the desk to fill out adoption paperwork, the shelter manager told him that she wouldn't adopt a dog to him because he was disabled, and therefore unable to properly care for a dog. "I was so crushed," explained Dennis. "I knew that I would take better care of a dog than anybody."

A few weeks later, he spotted a small terrier mix named Muffin at the Broward County Humane Society in Florida. It was love at first sight. "I called her, and she ran right over to me, jumped up in my lap and started licking my face," recalled Dennis. "That's all it took."

Although Dennis had been out on the golf course since his accident, it was quite difficult for him to hit balls from his wheelchair. "I wouldn't be out for long because I'd just get frustrated and go back inside. Muffin gave me the incentive I needed to stay at it. She was always there to offer moral support with a wag of her tail, or a kiss on the face. That meant so much to me."

A friend later rigged a special golf cart for Dennis that gave him the swiveling and hitting range he wasn't able to have in his wheelchair. Since golfing was what he loved most, he was determined to find a way to make a living at it. He remembered watching golf trick-shot artists on TV as a kid, and began practicing a few of the shots. With Muffin by his side, Dennis continued honing his trick-shot skills, and soon began giving small demonstrations in the area. In January 1977, he gave his first official performance for a crowd at the PGA Merchandise Show. Soon thereafter, the "Dennis Walter's Golf Show" was born.

During his one-hour show, Dennis hits balls blindfolded; he hits balls from under cups and from under an egg without cracking the shell;

he hits three balls at once with a "3 iron" club (three club heads welded together onto one handle); he hits a succession of rapid-fire shots, and his finale is a death-defying drive through flames.

For thirteen years, Muffin traveled the country with Dennis while he performed his amazing shows for thousands. "She just slept through all of my shows until the finale, then she'd wake up. When people

Dennis Walters and Mulligan

ask me what Muffin did in my shows, I tell them she did nothing—but she did it with class. She was a real lady," says Dennis. After Muffin died in 1991, Dennis was heartbroken. He later endowed an adoption room in her memory at the humane society from where she was adopted.

Dennis adopted his next dog, another terrier mix, from the Orlando Humane Society. He named the dog Mulligan, which means "second chance" in golf lingo. "She was my second dog, and it was also a second chance for her, so I figured that was the perfect name." He had Mulligan trained as a certified service dog in order to help him with tasks such as picking up dropped items, and retrieving things. He also taught her to tee-up a golf ball, and other tricks like waving, sitting up, and high-five, which she began performing at his shows.

Although Mulligan was more difficult to train, she reminded Dennis very much of Muffin. "I often thought she was like Muffin reincarnated. She looked almost exactly like her, and did some things that only Muffin would know how to do. Mulligan had such a great personality. She was so sweet and affectionate, and everyone loved her."

In October 1996, another horrible tragedy struck. Dennis and Mulligan were performing in Florida for a group of five hundred kids at Disney World. Mulligan was sitting about fifteen feet from Dennis as he was preparing for his last trick—hitting rapid-fire balls one after the other. When he was in mid-swing on the last ball, Mulligan unexpectedly bolted towards him. "Every time I close my eyes, I can hear the sound of her head hitting the club," recalls Dennis's sister, Barbara Herman, who accompanies him to his shows.

Mulligan was rushed to a nearby emergency vet clinic, where she hung on for two days hooked to life support. Finally, Dennis couldn't bear it anymore, and he cradled her in his arms, and gave her a tearful kiss goodbye. To this day, he's still not sure why Mulligan suddenly ran towards him. Her sudden and horrible death took a tremendous toll on Dennis. "I felt ill and couldn't sleep for two months afterwards. It's something I'll never get over."

Dennis dreaded the thought of searching for a new dog again, but he pushed himself to do it. Every day for almost two months, he visited animal shelters looking for a dog. He finally found the "perfect dog," a mutt, through a local rescue group. He named the dog Benji Hogan. Benji, because he's a dead-ringer for the famous movie dog, and Hogan after Dennis's favorite golfer, Ben Hogan. "Hogan is by far the smartest dog I've ever known," Dennis said proudly. So smart, that he amazes the greatest of golfers, celebrities, and crowds with his extraordinary talents.

At the beginning of each show Hogan performs his ten-minute routine. He waves hello to the crowd with his paw in the air; retrieves a Kleenex for Dennis when he sneezes; tees up a golf ball, and does several other tricks. But what really wows the audience is Hogan's incredible ability to do math problems, card tricks, and answer golf trivia questions by barking accordingly. "You can ask him just about anything. I think he's truly a mathematical genius," says Dennis.

During Hogan's performances, Dennis invites a few kids from the audience to come up and ask him questions. "He gets them right every time. The kids are always amazed." In fact, even Tiger Woods and other pro golfers are constantly amazed by Hogan's talents. "Tiger is always

Photo © Downtown Photo, Inc.

Hogan

trying to stump him, but hasn't been able to do it yet."

More than anything, Hogan is a cherished companion to Dennis. "Hogan is my little boy, and he knows I'm his dad." The two travel around the country, along with Dennis's sister Barbara, in a customized motor home, performing between eighty and a hundred shows a year. Dennis affectionately refers to Hogan as "the only touring pro from the Miami dog pound."

At each of Dennis's shows he always informs the audience that he adopted Hogan and his other dogs from shelters and encourages them to do the same. Every year he donates portions of the proceeds from his shows to local humane societies and performs for charity events at various shelters ❧

Violet Folsom

Dwane Folsom and Shadow

Shadow

EXPERT SCUBA DIVER

When scuba diving near his home in Florida, Dwane Folsom's wife Vi, and his dog Shadow, would always join him for the boat ride out to sea. One day, while out on a dive, Shadow suddenly jumped from the boat into the ocean, and began chasing Dwane's bubbles as they surfaced.

Dwane had tried for years to convince Vi to join him scuba diving, but after noticing Shadow's fascination with his hobby, he decided to see if Shadow could be his diving companion instead. After a year of tinkering in his garage and testing various devices, Dwane was able to create a workable scuba system for Shadow. He constructed her diving harness using parts from a diver's belt and used a UV-stabilized, clear plastic globe for her head gear. He then attached a seven-foot air hose to his oxygen tank to provide her air supply.

Dwane slowly introduced Shadow to her new diving gear, one piece at a time, to make sure she would be comfortable. After several practice sessions in the swimming pool and with the approval of Shadow's veterinarian, she was ready for her first ocean dive.

Six years later, with more than two hundred dives under her collar, Shadow has become an expert scuba diver. Along with Dwane, she has been diving in the West Indies, and the Cayman Islands, where she was issued her very own passport. A photo of Shadow scuba diving now hangs on a wall in Milan, Italy, with the caption reading: "We can teach anyone to dive!" As for Dwane, he is forever upgrading Shadow's scuba gear. His latest addition is an intercom system in Shadow's helmet so she can hear him underwater ❧

Shadow practices in the pool with Dwane Folsom.

Caution: Please do not attempt this with your dog. Most dogs would not enjoy activities such as scuba diving or boogie boarding. These sports can be dangerous for dogs as well as for humans.

Photo © Alan Sweetman

Tom and Bonnie Brackney and their "Mad Cap Mutts."

"Mad Cap Mutts" and "Mess of Mutts"
THE SHOW MUTTS GO ON

Little Susie is the singer of the bunch. Marty, a handsome fellow with big soft eyes, is the cheerleader. Then there's Scooter, who makes sure that nobody ever leaves his vicinity without first getting smothered with kisses. Along with Rusty, Holly, Sandy, Stormy, Minnie, Sally, Pepper and Amos, this bunch of scruffy dogs make up Tom and Bonnie Brackney's "Madcap Mutts"—a group of eleven canine comedians and acrobats.

The Madcap Mutts have performed internationally in numerous shows including *Holiday On Ice*, and on Broadway in the original production of *The Will Roger's Follies*. As their opening act demonstrates, all of the dogs were rescued from animal shelters. As each dog appears one by one through the mock animal shelter door on stage, the Brackneys proudly introduce their beloved mutts. They encourage audiences to save other dogs by adopting from animal shelters, and never let a show go by without mentioning the importance of spaying and neutering.

While the Brackney's mutts are working the East Coast, Bonnie's cousin, Stacy Moore and his "Mess of Mutts" are touring the West Coast. After perform-

Stacy Moore and Toby

ing at a California humane society fund raiser in 1989, Stacy became aware of the serious pet overpopulation problem and vowed to do something to help. Since then, he has adopted more than seventy dogs from animal shelters around the country. He recruited some of the dogs for his shows, and found homes for others who weren't cut out for show business.

"The main focus behind what I do, is just having fun with the dogs," explained Stacy. "They really enjoy learning these tricks, and enjoy working—it makes them feel more like part of the family." Amazingly, all ten of his dogs perform off-leash, doing everything from walking a tight rope to delivering letters in a mailbox. Like his cousins in the East, Stacy mentions that all of his mutts were adopted from animal shelters, and he encourages the audience to do the same.❧

Pete

JUST SAY WOOF TO DRUGS

With a single paw, "Officer Pete" has recovered several hundred thousand dollars in cash, and has been responsible for removing more than $4 million worth of drugs from the streets of Richmond, California. Pete, a lab mix, is a seven-year veteran of the Richmond Police Department, and a partner and best friend to Officer Rod Smith.

At the age of twelve, he's considered a canine senior citizen, but there are no plans for retirement in the near future. "Pete loves his job, he loves working and is in great shape for his age," says Rod. In fact, Pete competes regularly in K9 trials against other narcotic dogs, and has several awards and trophies under his collar. For the past four years in a row he has been named the Western States Police Canine Association champion narcotics dog, beating out many of his purebred competitors.

More Amazing Mutts

Claudia
THE MUTT WHO "DIDN'T LEAVE HOME WITHOUT IT"

In November 1990, Claudia Farber of Sausalito, California got just what she was waiting for to do her holiday shopping. An American Express card in her name arrived in the mail, with a $5,000 credit line and a welcome letter from the company. Her parents were quite surprised by this, especially since Claudia was their sixteen year old mixed-breed dog, who had passed away several months earlier. They were properly mystified since neither of them has an American Express card, or had ever applied for one.

Coco
THE CANINE CASTAWAY

In August 1998, a lab and chow mix named Coco set off to sea with her owners Andrew Block and Julie Parsons. The three had planned a leisurely trip through the Gulf of Mexico aboard their twenty-nine-foot sailboat.

Everything was smooth sailing until a freak wave washed Andrew and Julie overboard as they were showering in the stern of the moving boat. Coco, stunned by the event, stayed in the boat watching as her owners drifted further and further away.

After treading naked in the water for twenty hours, the exhausted couple was finally rescued by a Coast Guard helicopter, but the boat carrying Coco was nowhere in sight. Once the word got out, calls came in from dog lovers all over Tampa Bay concerned about Coco's welfare. Private donations and volunteer pilots launched an airborne search-and-rescue mission for the dog lost at sea.

After four days alone at sea, Coco was finally found by a fisher who noticed the drifting boat with only a dog aboard. Coco was extremely thirsty, but apparently had been sleeping in the shade of the cabin and dining on snack foods.

It was deemed as nothing short of a miracle that Coco was able to survive the ordeal and come out in such good shape. A few hours after she was found, Coco was happily reunited with her family❧

Nikki

THIRTY-MILE A DAY MUTT

Each morning when Nikki Alexander's school bus arrived, she headed off to school in Eaglesville, Tennessee. This normally wouldn't appear to be unusual, except that Nikki is a dog. Instead of boarding the bus, she ran behind it for the fifteen-mile trip to school. There was a very special reason for Nikki's unusual attraction to the school bus—her young companion, Cory, was aboard, and she wanted to be sure he made it safely to school each day. Rain or shine, there was Nikki, trailing close behind the bus as it made its daily journey.

Once the bus arrived at school and let everyone off, Nikki would wait patiently outside the gate until school was out and it was time for Cory to go home. Then off she went for her fifteen-mile jog back home, behind the bus. Word began to spread about Nikki's daily thirty-mile trips, and before long, stories appeared on CNN, in the *National Enquirer*, and in other newspapers across the country.

Eventually, Cory's mother, Lisa, decided it would be safer to keep Nikki at home. A local dog lover was so impressed by Nikki's story that he donated money for the Alexanders to fence their yard❧

Brownie
CHURCH-GOING MUTT

In 1993, a stray dog wandered into Reverend Richard McCue's backyard in Spruce Pine, North Carolina. The kindly priest took in the malnourished dog, fattened him up, and named him Brownie. McCue began taking Brownie with him to Sunday morning Mass. At first Brownie was only allowed in the back of the congregation, but eventually he began joining McCue at the pulpit, and became the first altar mutt at St. Lucien Catholic Church. A photo of Brownie in church appeared in the *National Enquirer* with the caption "let us all bow-wow down❧"

Abby
THE TREE CLIMBER

One day Jimmy Smith of Tallahassee, Florida was enjoying a cold beer after work and tucked the bottle in a nearby tree for a moment. Without Smith saying a word, his dog Abby went over to the tree, looked up at the bottle, and quickly pawed her way several feet up the tree to retrieve it. From then on, fetching beer bottles from trees became a regular hobby for the shepherd mix. Smith figured if Abby was smart enough to do that, she might even be smart enough to count. He was right. Abby quickly learned to add and subtract by barking the right number of times when prompted❧

Sandie

THE SURROGATE MOTHER

In Auburn Maine, a mutt named Sandie took over mothering duties for four newborn kittens when the mother cat, Badger, was unable to feed her babies. Sandie's owner, Dot Hutchinson, was not really surprised by Sandie's actions, since Sandie was raised by a cat herself.

Timex

BACK FROM THE DEAD

In August 1998, at an animal shelter in Uniontown, Pennsylvania, a young lab mix whom no one wanted to adopt was euthanized by lethal injection, then put in the freezer with other euthanized cats and dogs.

The following day, a shelter worker went to unload the freezer. He thought he was seeing things when the same dog that should have been dead came walking out alive! The dog was rushed to a local vet who said it was nothing short of a miracle that he had survived being in deep freeze for almost twenty-four hours!

Two of the shelter staff vowed to find a home for this special dog, who had such an incredible will to survive. They named the dog Timex. Once word got out about Timex's story, dozens of people came forward to offer him a new home. Shortly thereafter, Timex was placed with a family that owns a big farm where he has lots of room to run and play.

Gary Gardetto

Beaks

HANGING TWENTY

Gary Gardetto's favorite pastime is boogie boarding in the beautiful waters off of Kailua, Hawaii, where he lives. However, he never imagined that his dog, Beaks would also take up his hobby.

After moving to Hawaii from California, Gary began frequenting the beach near his home to enjoy boogie boarding. For the first several weeks, Beaks watched and waited patiently on the shore while Gary was hanging-ten in the water. Then one day, to Gary's utter amazement, Beaks dove into the ocean, swam up to Gary's board that was floating near by, and tried to pull himself up onto the board. Gary helped Beaks onto the board and helped him to gain his balance. Before long Beaks was hanging-twenty all on his own. Gary has since bought Beaks his very own boogie board, and the two of them now enjoy their favorite pastime together❀

Benji

— CHAPTER SIX —

Mutt Celebrities

*O*ver the past few decades an increasing number of movies, TV shows, and commercials have featured mutts. Hollywood has begun to recognize the unique qualities of mutts, which has encouraged animal trainers to turn to animal shelters when searching for their next canine star. As a result, the public is also encouraged to adopt from an animal shelter when looking for a new canine companion.

Benji is probably the most widely recognized mutt celebrity, but there have been many other mutts who have followed in his famous paw prints. Featured in this chapter are some of the most popular mutt celebrities past and present.

◆ ◆ ◆

Benji

One of the most memorable experiences I had while writing this book, was meeting Frank Inn, the man who "discovered" Benji, and several other mutt celebrities. Frank graciously welcomed me into his home in Southern California, where we talked for several hours about his incredible experiences as a Hollywood animal trainer. He shared with me his wall-to-wall photo albums, filled with countless pictures and memorabilia of Benji and other famous animal stars dating back more than forty years. I also had the great pleasure of meeting Benji III, and listening to

Courtesy of Frank Inn

Benji and Frank Inn

Frank read a few of the touching poems he has written about Benji and some of his other animal stars.

Frank found the original Benji (really named Higgins) at the animal shelter in Burbank, California, the day before Higgins was scheduled for euthanasia. He immediately recognized star qualities in the scruffy terrier mix, and knew he would someday "make his mark" in Hollywood.

Higgins began his acting career as a regular on the TV series "Petticoat Junction." After seven successful years on the show, he retired at the age of thirteen. But not for long. The studios approached Frank to have Higgins star in *Benji*—the first movie to ever feature a mutt in the leading role.

Although Higgins was a canine senior citizen at the time, Frank knew he was up for the challenge. The first *Benji* movie premiered in 1978, grossing an incredible $100 million. Unfortunately Higgins didn't have much of a chance to enjoy his overnight fame, since he died shortly after the movie's release.

Benji II (Higgins's daughter) carried on her father's legacy, starring in five *Benji* sequels, and appearing in more than one hundred television shows over the next twelve years. Benji soon became a household name, and everything from stuffed Benji dogs to board games could be found in stores across the country. Frank and Benji made appearances for adoring fans around the world, and received the red-carpet treatment wherever they traveled.

Benji was certainly Frank's most famous animal star, but not the only one. His house is decorated with numerous Patsy Awards—an award given to animal actors that is comparable to an Oscar. His other animal stars include Arnold the pig from the sitcom "Green Acres," and Tramp, the shaggy terrier mix featured on the sitcom "My Three Sons."

"Benji was a great spokesdog for mutts everywhere," noted Frank. "I believe his fame and popularity made a big difference by motivating people to adopt dogs from a shelter. To this day I still hear people refer to various terrier mixes as a 'Benji dog,' but of course there is no such breed."

Frank and Benji III currently give live performances for the elderly and for disabled children at his home in Southern California. A documentary chronicling Frank's fifty-plus years as a Hollywood animal trainer is presently in the works, along with a book.

Tramp and Ernie from the sitcom "My Three Sons."

Courtesy of Karl Miller

Leo from the TV series "Tales of the Gold Monkey."

Leo and Scruffy

Karl Lewis Miller is one of the most sought after animal trainers in Hollywood today. One of his most famous protégés is a St. Bernard named Chris, who played Beethoven in the hit movies. Karl was also the head trainer for more than nine hundred animals in the movie *Babe*, and the sequel: *Babe: Pig in the City*.

Karl has worked with hundreds of dogs during his thirty-plus year career, but he has always had a special place in his heart for mutts. One of his favorites was a bull terrier mix named Leo. Leo was best known for his role as the one-eyed canine sidekick Jack, on a series called "Tales of the Gold Monkey" in the early 1980s. By the time Leo had landed that role, he was a nine-year veteran actor with numerous television and film credits, including a recurring role as a camp dog on the hit TV series "M*A*S*H."

Leo was discovered in the Miami Humane Society by another animal trainer who turned the dog over to Karl when he moved to

Courtesy of Karl Miller

Scruffy and his co-stars from the TV series "The Ghost and Mrs. Muir."

California. Leo started out as just another dog in Karl's kennel, but the lovable mutt quickly won his way into Miller's heart and home. "He was much more than just a working dog, he was a cherished member of our family, and my constant companion," Karl explained. "At night he slept in the bed between me and my wife, and sometimes even tried to push me out. Whenever we were watching TV or reading, he was either in my wife's lap, or curled up at my feet," recalled Karl.

Another one of Karl's favorite dogs was the mutt appropriately named Scruffy who starred in the TV series, "The Ghost and Mrs. Muir," in the late 1960s. The terrier mix lived at the Miller's home along with Leo, and was "one of the smartest dogs." He was so smart that he even mastered the game of chess, well sort-of. "He kind of pushed the chess pieces around with his paws and acted like he knew what he was doing for his role," Karl reminisced, laughing.

Courtesy of Thompson Consumer Electronics

Nipper, the RCA mascot (left), and his sidekick, Chipper.

Nipper

Flying first class, riding in limousines, and signing "paw-tographs" for fans is just par for the course these days for Nipper, the famous RCA mascot and spokesdog.

But life has not always been on easy street for Nipper. He was saved from certain death by animal trainer, Bambi Brook, who rescued him from a company that was selling animals for medical research. She took him to the Dawn Animal Agency, a sanctuary in New York for animals in distress, where he was trained for commercials.

After noticing the striking resemblance to the original RCA Nipper from 1929, the new Nipper was chosen to launch an ad campaign for the company. Nipper's earnings are donated to help some of his less-fortunate animal friends at the Dawn Agency's 250-acre sanctuary that is home to more than eight hundred rescued animals. Nipper's best friend at the sanctuary is a little dog named Pup-Pup who was found as a stray.

Just like every actor, Nipper gets made up for his roles. Makeup is applied to darken his ears and spots, and he's powdered to look and feel good. He's always very relaxed on the set, and often takes dog naps while waiting for his cues. But when called to action, Nipper is ready to roll, sometimes literally.

Nipper also has a stand-in waiting in the wings, but an exact replacement can never be found because he's a mutt! His sidekick, Chipper, is played by rotating Jack Russell terrier pups.

Being a celebrity dog of the hi-tech times, Nipper has his own web site called "Nipperscape" featuring a complete history of how the original Nipper came to be, along with other interesting facts and photos.

Internet users can log onto: http://www.ais.org/~lsa/nipper.html

Courtesy of Thompson Consumer Electronics

Portrait of the original Nipper from 1929.

©1995 Columbia Tristar Television

Murray

Murray is one of the most popular canine actors today, with his fan mail rivaling that of Eddie, the dog on TV's "Frasier." The handsome collie mix, who plays the part of an airhead-type on the sitcom "Mad About You, was rescued from the Castaic animal shelter near Los Angeles more than ten years ago. Murray made his debut on the show during its first season in 1992, and has been one of the main characters ever since. Like most famous stars, Murray is only his stage name—his real name is Maui❧

Magic

What a face! That's what I said when I saw the photo of Magic that appears on the cover of this book. Magic was adopted from an animal shelter in Northern California by Bow Wow Productions. She is currently under contract as the mascot for Old Navy Clothing stores, and a line of clothing and products bearing her likeness have become a huge hit with Old Navy customers.

The airedale terrier mix has also starred in numerous commercials, including Fuji Film, Ford, and Bank of America, and she has appeared in more than thirty theatrical shows and magazine ads. Bow, hide your eyes, answer the phone, limp, hit a mark, and go kiss are among more than fifty behaviors Magic can perform on cue.

FX Pet Department

Talk show host, Steve Walker, and his co-host, Jack.

Jack

A terrier mix named Jack is the only known canine co-host featured on a talk show. Along with his co-host and companion, Steve Walker, Jack appears every day on the FX channel's "Pet Department." During the half-hour show Jack "interviews" celebrity guests and their pets, and plays host to a variety of animal guests, including dogs, cats, birds, and reptiles.

Jack's path to stardom began out of near tragedy. He was a stray pup crossing a New York City street when he was hit by a bus. Thanks to the efforts of one compassionate woman, the ASPCA, and a kind veterinarian, Jack was nursed back to health. He was put up for adoption at the ASPCA shelter, which is where he and Steve met.

Courtesy of Gary Gero

Freddie

Freddie is best known for his recurrent role in all of the *Back to the Future* films. The briard mix has also been featured in several commercials and has made guest appearances on television shows including "Family Matters" and "Dear John." Freddie was discovered by trainer, Gary Gero, in a shelter in Orange County, California. Gary has launched the careers of many other mutt celebrities, including a St. Bernard and retriever mix named Bear who played the lovable Dryfus on "The Empty Nest" TV series❧

Penny

— CHAPTER SEVEN—

Mutts Who Lend a Helping Paw

*F*or people who are physically disabled, dogs have proven time and again to be a human's best friend. From retrieving money at an instant teller machine, to carrying bags of groceries, specially trained service dogs have enabled thousands of physically impaired people to live fairly active lives.

Most guide dogs today are purebred labs or golden retrievers, but when it comes to hearing dogs, mutts are truly all ears. They have proven to be the quickest learners and have the best temperaments to assist the hearing impaired. Thousands of dogs have been rescued from shelters around the country and recruited by organizations that train them to assist the deaf or hearing impaired.

Hearing dogs perform a variety of tasks for their guardians, in some instances alerting them to life-threatening situations such as fire alarms. Since the deaf cannot hear a dog's bark, the dogs use other methods of getting attention, such as jumping up against the person, then running to the source of the sound.

Dogs of all shapes and sizes, purebred or mutt, have been successfully used as therapy, service, and hearing dogs. The following stories are a small sampling of mutts who lend a helping paw and a healing heart.

Penny

AN OFFICIAL SPOKESDOG

In 1979, an abandoned six-month old puppy was brought to the San Francisco SPCA. While waiting for a new home, staff members from the SPCA's Hearing Dog Program recruited the puppy for their very first class. Her sweet disposition and eagerness to please made her a prime candidate for the program. They named her Penny.

Penny proved to be a star pupil, and graduated as top dog in her class. The staff was so impressed with Penny's abilities and charming personality, they voted to give her a permanent home at the SPCA as the official "Demo Dog" for the Hearing Dog Program.

For more than fifteen years Penny traveled the country giving demonstrations. Like a true ambassador, she visited schools, pet shows, organizations for the hearing impaired, and animal welfare groups, demonstrating the many tasks that hearing dogs assist their guardians with.

Penny became quite a celebrity. Her photo appeared in *Time*, *Newsweek*, and *National Geographic*, and at one time or another, she was profiled on every one of the San Francisco Bay area's TV stations. She also holds the distinction of being the only dog ever to leap atop a pitcher's mound at Candlestick Park, as she showed her stuff to a cheering crowd at a San Francisco Giant's game in 1988.

Penny was loved by everyone at the SPCA, especially the Hearing Dog Program Director, Ralph Dennard, who took her home with him each night. "I knew Penny was special the first time I saw her in our adoption kennels. There was a bright sparkle in those devilish terrier eyes that simply won my heart instantly," recalled Ralph. After her retirement in 1992, Ralph formally adopted Penny, and even though she was officially retired, she still insisted on accompanying Ralph to work every day.

In the summer of 1996, Penny died at the age of seventeen. "Penny was not purebred, but she was pure joy. She was a great worker and a wonderful companion, and I feel very lucky to have had her in my life for over seventeen years," said Ralph❧

Sunny
A HALL OF FAMER
–Terri Nash

Terri Nash and Sunny

When I adopted Sunny, I had no idea that one dog could fulfill so many of my known and unknown needs. I have multiple sclerosis and my physical condition will worsen as time goes on. As I write this from my wheelchair, the pages come off the laser printer, and Sunny brings them to me one by one. She is so gentle with her mouth that she can retrieve the pages without putting any teeth marks or saliva on them. This is only one of the countless tasks Sunny performs for me on a daily basis.

I rescued Sunny from the SPCA more than nine years ago. She was about ten months old at the time, and had been brought to the shelter by her previous owners because she proved to be a supreme escape artist. I was very lucky to stumble upon her, as she had already been at the shelter for ten days, and was on the "short list" (I think you know what I mean).

Sunny was a challenge from the start, but after having trained horses and dogs for many years, I knew that a few months of the right training could do wonders. Little did I know at the time, that I'd really struck gold with Sunny. In less than a year, she learned more than a hundred commands, and continues to learn new ones all of the time. Her vocabulary comprehension is about the equivalent of a two-year old child.

Sunny helps me with numerous tasks every day: She turns lights on and off; opens and shuts doors; pulls my wheelchair with me in it; and when we come home in the car, she jumps out to retrieve my "downstairs" wheelchair. She can pick up almost anything, from a coin to a credit card dropped on the floor, and can carry an apple to me without even breaking the skin! She routinely shuttles things up and down the stairs in my home, which saves me an immeasurable amount of time. In our tiny kitchen, she opens and shuts the refrigerator door, flips up the dishwasher door, and loves to put empty cans in the recycle bin.

At the office, Sunny delivers papers and mail so I don't have to adjust my position, and at the flip of her paw, she brings the footrest up or down on my wheelchair. When we're out shopping or running errands, Sunny pulls when I need assistance, and helps carry packages to and from the car. I have never forced Sunny to do anything she doesn't want to, which is why I believe she is so willing to help. We've established a deep bond and trust between us.

Not only does Sunny help me with so many physical things that are difficult for me to accomplish, but she also is a great help to me mentally and emotionally. As much as Sunny helps me, I also feel responsible for her well being, which gives me a much needed sense of accomplishment, especially when the rest of my life is crumbling around me. I love the attention she draws when we're out in public, and we'll always stop to meet and talk with people who are interested in her. Sunny, of course, loves the attention too.

Sunny and I have been frequently featured as a classic human interest story in local newspapers and on TV, starting with her reign as "Homecoming Queen" for the Monterey County SPCA in 1989. She has won numerous awards in recognition for her outstanding service, including her 1991 induction into the California Veterinary Association Animal Hall of Fame for "Steadfast Devotion to Duty." In 1997, Sunny was honored as the first inductee into the Mixed Breed Dog Club of America's Dog Hall of Fame. All of this from a four-legger who almost had her lights snuffed out because she wouldn't stay home!

Photo © Larry Stanley, Stanley Photography

Ellen Raines and Meko

Meko

MY EARS

—Ellen Raines

For years I hid my hearing loss because I felt ashamed. As a child, I was labeled retarded, and was constantly rejected by my peers because of my handicap. It was very painful for me. I dreamed about being freed from my silent prison and having people look up to me, instead of down at me.

In my junior high school days I hid my handicap by becoming an excellent lip reader. I purposely never learned to sign so I could fool people into thinking I was able to hear. This made it easier for me to deny my deafness to others and to myself.

By the time I was eighteen, I was married with two children, but divorced shortly thereafter. My glass world of protection and love was shattered. I felt so isolated and alone, and sank into a deep depression. I became a recluse, hiding in my own home. I felt like I was a picture hanging on the wall, just a display and not moving. Due to my condition, my parents felt it would be best for my children to live with them. I felt like I had no control over my life or myself, it was such a helpless feeling.

But I realized I did have a choice—either keep sinking deeper into depression, or try to live a normal life and accept my deafness. My choice was to take action. I had heard about "hearing dogs" from some reading I had done, so I applied for a dog through an organization called Dogs for the Deaf in Oregon.

In June 1987 I received my new hearing dog named Meko. When I first saw her, I thought I had just made the biggest mistake of my life. Here was this short-haired dog with the biggest radar ears I'd ever seen, and she weighed only twelve pounds. She looked like a cross between a dachshund, a terrier, and a bat! I'd envisioned a much different type of dog, not a scruffy little mutt.

The first few days were a bit awkward for both of us, but by the end of the first week we were feeling a lot more comfortable with each other. Meko began alerting me to the phone, the door bell, and other sounds such as police or ambulance sirens while I was driving. Her favorite sound is the toaster. She loves to watch the toast pop up and lets me know right away so it never gets cold.

I needed to take Meko out for her daily walks, so I was forced out of the isolation in my home. Slowly I began to come out of my shell, and started realizing the positive impact that Meko was having on my life. But things were not easy for us. People in my home town of Billings, Montana were not familiar with hearing dogs, so we were run out of many stores and other public places.

In November 1990, I went with some friends to a nice restaurant for dinner. The restaurant owner greeted us, and I showed him Meko's ID and the booklet of state laws for hearing dogs. He refused to listen or look at the booklet, and said, "Customers will complain. My customers come first, not dogs!" My friends and I were humiliated. I was so angry afterwards, I felt like he was telling me that my ears are not allowed in his restaurant. That incident was a real turning point for me. Finally I admitted to myself that not only did I have to fight for Meko's rights, but for mine too. Meko is my ears, she is part of me as a whole.

My mother describes my behavior before and after Meko, as like having two daughters. Meko helped change me from a once-shy recluse to an outgoing advocate for the rights of hearing dogs and their guardians. We began giving public demonstrations at various schools and organizations to educate people about hearing dogs. Speaking up for Meko's rights gave me a new purpose in life and a new outlook. I began to feel proud of her, and proud of myself for fighting for what I believed was right.

In the fall of 1994, Meko nudged me to alert me to the phone ringing. As I read my special phone screen, (for the hearing-impaired) I was in disbelief. It said: "Congratulations, Meko has been chosen as Hearing Dog of the Year!" I cried with joy. That October, Meko received her award from the Delta Society, an organization that promotes the bond between pets and people. As the medal was placed around her neck, I almost burst with pride. The dog that I once thought was just an ugly mutt had become the most wonderful and beautiful dog in the world to me!

The changes in my life since I've had Meko are phenomenal. She drew me out of the depths of despair and helped me to change my outlook on life and myself. When I stopped rejecting myself for my deafness, my heart became so full of love for Meko, my ears, and myself. Now I can love me for who I am. Today, I am proud to say, "I am deaf."

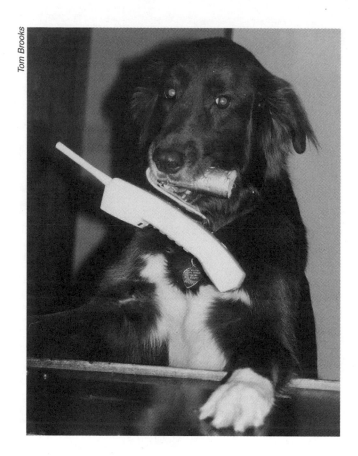

Tom Brooks

Maggie

A BEST FRIEND

For fifteen years attendants helped Frank Champagne to dress, cook his meals, and drive him to doctor appointments and other errands. But now he has Maggie, a brown-and-white lab mix. Maggie can't cook for him or drive his car, but she helps him with many other tasks that he is unable to perform.

Frank lost the use of his arms and legs while on the job in January 1982. A large chunk of frozen sludge slid through the tailgate of a nineteen-ton dump truck as he was emptying it, instantly breaking his neck. Despite more than nine months at a rehabilitation facility, he remained

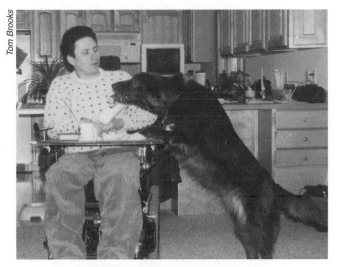

Frank Champagne and Maggie

permanently paralyzed. "One minute you can walk, the next minute you can't. It was very scary for me at first, and it took me quite a while to get used to an entirely different way of life," explained Frank. "Even though I had people around helping me, I still experienced days of feeling lonely and isolated."

A friend of Frank's had seen a documentary featuring an organization called Paws With a Cause located in nearby Grand Rapids, Michigan. This organization rescues shelter dogs from around the country and trains them as special service dogs for people with various disabilities. The caring friend immediately phoned Frank to tell him about it, and offered to pay the $8,500 sponsorship fee for one of the dogs. Frank readily accepted the generous offer, and in February 1996 he received Maggie.

In the past few years since Maggie came along, Frank's life has changed dramatically. "Not only does Maggie help me with every task imaginable, but she can always sense if I'm feeling down, and will come over and lay her head on my lap," explained Frank. "It makes me just forget all of my troubles. She's the best thing that's happened to me, and without a doubt, my absolute best friend!" ❧

Carol-Joan Calfapietra

Billy-Bob with a group of his favorite students.

Billy-Bob
A GENTLE GIANT
—Carol-Joan Calfapietra

Billy-Bob is definitely our most popular teacher among the five hundred children at the Special Services School in Cape May, New Jersey. Disabilities range from severe physical problems to children who are emotionally disturbed. Billy is like a gentle giant who somehow senses the children's different needs, and adapts his behavior accordingly. With the fragile children, he is gentle; with a child who is upset and losing control, he gives kisses; and with children who are lonely, he gives friendship.

Students who cannot speak, often work with a large tactile squeaky ball that helps them learn cause and effect, such as squeeze the ball and emit the sound. When they do this Billy comes to them. Students who are rigid or tactile resistant, become relaxed by listening to Billy's breathing or his heartbeat. Students who have difficulty controlling themselves are brought to Billy as a crisis intervention technique. After a short walk with Billy, or just by sitting and petting him, the child will usually calm down.

Billy is wonderful at helping the children's self-esteem. When a child walks him on the leash, and he responds to their commands: "Billy, forward; Billy, halt; Billy left," they feel a great sense of accomplishment. One student was able to teach Billy how to drink from the classroom water fountain on command. Billy is truly an angel for these children. It's amazing how the unconditional love of one dog can help so many children in need❀

Splotch

A HEALING SPIRIT

—In Splotch's words as told to: Julie Miller

I have the best job in the world. I motivate sick people to get better, and help make them laugh and smile when they're sad or lonely. I'm a therapy dog and my name is Splotch. I live with another therapy dog named Pita. She's a purebred lab, and thinks she is top dog when it comes to therapy. But I know that mutts are the best medicine for what ails, so I let Pita indulge herself in her delusions.

My therapy assistant is my human mom, Julie. Together we volunteer once a week at a rehabilitation hospital and an acute care hospital. And every couple of months we go to a psychiatric prison to visit the inmates. I've had some wonderful experiences as a therapy dog, and I can tell by watching Julie that what we do really makes a difference. She is a critical care nurse and many times I've seen her eyes mist with tears when we help someone gain back his or her life. Here are a few of my most memorable experiences as a therapy dog.

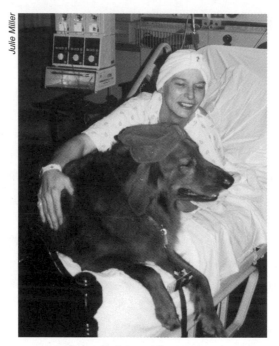

Julie Miller

Splotch visits with a patient.

One time at the acute care hospital, we entered a dimly lit room where an emaciated man lay in bed. His family thought he'd like to see me, so they helped him sit up to pet me. I sat next to his bed and watched him smile as he scratched my ears. I overheard his family tell Julie that he wasn't expected to live more than another week. The man thanked me for coming, and his family told Julie that it was so important for him to say good-bye to an animal, as he had loved animals all of his life.

At the rehabilitation hospital we often work with stroke victims who are trying to regain their speech. There is no sweeter music to my ears than when I hear a patient speak my name, after weeks, sometimes months without talking. At the prison the inmates love to play fetch with me, but my favorite part is when they pet me and tell me that it has been years since they last touched an animal.

I have many memories of patients who I have seen during my four years of therapy work. To see a smile light up a patient's face when I enter the room. To feel the touch of a hand from a young man who is paralyzed, and to know I motivated him to move that hand for the first time. To snuggle close to an unconscious trauma victim, and feel him reach out to scratch my fur. To hear my name from a patient relearning to talk after cancer stole his voice box. To retrieve the ball that the head-injured patient threw for me for the first time. To watch a child smile through her tears as I play high five. To feel the strain of the waiting room melt away as I spend time with the families of the critically ill. To make such a difference in so many lives is the greatest reward of being a therapy dog. And I know one day when I die, I'll once again be rejoined with the many wonderful friends I've made here on earth.

Reggie
A LIFELINE TO FREEDOM
—Mary Rook

When we first found Reggie, he was flea infested, suffering from severe ear infections, and was very fearful of people. He was clearly someone's "throwaway dog." But with lots of love and patience, the real personality of this marvelous animal began to emerge.

I have multiple sclerosis, and from the start Reggie seemed to notice that I moved around differently from the rest of the family. He somehow knew that I needed assistance, and communicated to me his willingness to help. When we decided to keep Reggie, we had never intended to use him as my aide dog. But after noticing how interested he was in helping me, we decided to send him for special training at a nearby facility. Reggie was a very quick learner and graduated at the top of his class.

Today, Reggie is my constant companion, my lifeline to the world that others walk through freely. I no longer have to wait for family or friends to take me places. Whenever I need to go somewhere, Reggie is always ready. With his help I can get up and down stairs again. He stead-ies me when I'm unbalanced by jostling crowds, and picks up things that

Scott Rook

Reggie helps Mary Rook do her grocery shopping.

I drop. If I fall down I don't have to ask a stranger to help me. Using my cane, and Reggie's willing shoulders, I can stand up again.

Reggie has come such a long way from his fearful, cowering days. Today he is a proud canine ambassador for the Northwest Aide Dog Foundation. Together we visit schools throughout the Pacific Northwest, educating students about aide dogs. In July 1995, Reggie accepted an Aide Dog Awareness Month proclamation from Governor Mike Lowry, in honor of aide dogs in Washington State. And Reggie was invited to "throw out" the first pitch at a Seattle Mariner's game. Amazing to think that someone just discarded Reggie like a worthless piece of garbage—perhaps because he didn't have a pedigree. Their loss has definitely been my gain. To me Reggie is the most priceless dog and wonderful mutt in the world❧

Shelley Graves

Jason Graves and Beamer

Beamer

INDEPENDENCE IN THE KEY OF "C"

At the age of three, a high fever left Jason Graves deaf in one ear. Then in 1993, a condition doctors call "sudden deafness," struck Jason's left ear, leaving him totally deaf at the age of nineteen. He was in his sophomore year as a music composition major at Appalachian's School of Music in North Carolina.

Many adjustments had to be made in order for Jason to continue with his studies. As a percussionist, he began to play barefoot to feel the music's vibrations through the floor and his professors had to alter some of the course work for him. In his apartment, he bought a vibrating alarm clock to place under his pillow at night, and he connected his phone and doorbell to a flickering light system.

Jason's parents became concerned for his safety, fearing the thought of a fire breaking out while he was at home, or while he was practicing alone at the campus music center. After researching various options, they learned about hearing dogs, and contacted several organizations. Most had long waiting lists, and some organizations charged up to $10,000 for a hearing dog.

Jason's younger sister was growing impatient and decided to take matters into her own hands. She secretly wrote a letter to the "Leeza" show after hearing about its "Grant a Wish" program. She asked the show's producer to please grant her wish to get a hearing dog for her brother.

Several months later, Jason and his family flew to California for what he thought was a free trip they had won to see a taping of the "Leeza" show. About ten minutes into the show, Leeza came over and asked Jason's family to join her on stage. Moments later, a small white-and-brown dog trotted on stage, and was presented to a very surprised Jason as his new hearing dog, Beamer.

The timing couldn't have been more perfect, especially for Beamer. The Benji-looking terrier mix was rescued by an organization called Paws With a Cause, just a half hour before he was scheduled to be euthanized. After three months of training at the group's Michigan headquarters, he became a certified hearing dog, and was sent home with Jason to Raleigh, North Carolina.

One of the first things Jason did after getting Beamer, was to get rid of the annoying alarm clock he had been sleeping with under his pillow. His new alarm clock proved to be much more pleasant with a few licks on the face each morning when it was time for class. Beamer began to alert Jason to the phone ringing, a knock on the door, or other noises he needed to be aware of.

Donning his special hearing dog identification vest and leash, Beamer accompanied Jason to class each day, where he became a familiar fixture on campus. He seemed to enjoy Jason's music, and would sit by his side as he practiced and composed. Beamer even became the official mascot for the Steely Pan Steele Band, which Jason played in.

In June 1996, Jason graduated with a degree in Music Composition. Later that year he married his longtime girlfriend, Ellen. She had been there when Beamer first arrived and was very involved in working with him and Jason. Ellen tried to convince Jason to have Beamer as the ring bearer at their wedding, but Jason would only agree to having him at the reception.

The following year, Jason was accepted into a special one-year program at the University of Southern California (USC) for TV film and scoring, and he, Ellen, and Beamer moved to California. Once again, Beamer accompanied Jason to campus each day, and sat by his side as he practiced. It was much easier going out in public with Beamer there because Californians were more accustomed to hearing dogs in public then people in North Carolina. After Jason received his certification for the program, he was hired almost immediately to write music scores for TV and films. At one point, Jason's credit line was appearing in five different TV shows.

The Hollywood life got to be old very fast, and Jason missed being near his family. So a year later they moved back home, and he got a job writing music scores for a multimedia production company. Jason was recently fitted with a digital hearing aid, which has dramatically increased his hearing ability. Although Beamer isn't as active working for Jason, he is still a treasured part of the family and always there to lend a good ear to Jason's music❖

Midnight
DOCTOR ON CALL
—Helen Muller

We keep telling visitors the story of how we adopted this sixty-pound black lab mix. In reality, Midnight adopted us—the residents and staff of Menorah Nursing Home in Brooklyn, New York.

Five years ago Midnight appeared on our grounds out of nowhere. He began escorting staff to and from the bus stop, but he was a fearful dog and kept his distance. Eventually he began to let the residents get close enough to touch and pet him, and he began regular visits with them. After a clean bill of health from the veterinarian, Midnight became a permanent "staff member" at the home.

Midnight has become a potent form of medicine at the nursing home. Recently a new resident to our home arrived, downcast and sad. But when I introduced her to Midnight, her entire demeanor changed. She sat upright in her wheelchair, reached out to Midnight and began to pet, caress, and talk to him.

Visitors are often amazed that Midnight has learned to navigate the elevators and travels floor to floor, visiting residents and nurses on duty. He has become a cherished member of the Menorah family, and brings joy and happiness to all our lives ❖

❖ ❖ ❖

"There is no better medicine than a dog licking your face."

ANONYMOUS

The ARC of Mecklenburg County, North Carolina

Daisy with one of her students, Kristen Wilkes.

Daisy

TEACHER AND FACULTY MEMBER

–Kathy Fallin

Easter had just passed, and school was out for a week. Life should have been good. Instead, my personal life was in ruin and my best friend, my pal, my confidant, developed an auto-immune disease. After three nights and four days in the animal hospital, I brought my schnauzer, Mugsy, home for one last night.

The next day, after Mugsy's funeral, I saw an ad in the paper for a workshop for grief-stricken pet owners. Somehow I managed to make it to the workshop that night—a workshop that changed my life. That night important friendships were made and new goals developed. I was determined that Mugsy's love and devotion would not be in vain. Goal number one was that somehow the students at the school where I worked—Metro School, a school for the mentally and physically dis-abled—would be able to experience the same special love and devotion that I had been blessed with through Mugsy.

Through the efforts of my co-workers, and many others who believed in my dream, we raised enough money to purchase a trained service dog for the school. Southeastern Dog Assistance in Greenville, South Carolina, had just the dog for us—a shaggy long-haired dog with a heart of gold named Daisy. Daisy also had a difficult past. She was found abandoned beside a highway where she sat refusing to leave a litter mate that had been hit by a car.

After extensive training for Daisy as well as the Metro School staff and parents, she arrived to a "Daisy Day" school-wide assembly. She was greeted with a very warm welcome that included proclamations, skits, music, posters, presents, and songs from the kids. Daisy became an official Metro School faculty member.

This long-haired teacher is versed in sign language and verbal com-mands as well as spatial concepts (on, off, front, back, around, over, under, etc.). Daisy enables students with poor gross motor skills to inde-pendently walk to other points in the school or independent students to walk without teacher intervention. Occupational and physical therapy goals are more easily achieved with Daisy's help. Students learn groom-ing skills, animal care and safety, as well as improving fine motor skills by brushing Daisy's fur or teeth.

In addition, self-esteem, motivation, and language skills have great-ly increased in many students because of their interactions with Daisy. Even when it comes to learning reading and arithmetic, Daisy is the perfect assistant. Students use bean bags and picture cards, which they stick with Velcro to Daisy's sides. When we're teaching colors, Daisy will wear her red coat or other colored clothing.

Just like the other teachers, Daisy receives birthday cards and letters written to her by the students. Watching Daisy with the kids is like watching miracles occur before my very eyes on a daily basis. One stu-dent had a choice of either wearing glasses or facing further eye surgery. After refusing to wear the glasses for three days, he finally agreed to wear them so he could walk with Daisy. Another student, who is severely retarded and responds to very little, cries if he can't be near Daisy. The list goes on and on.

I reflect back on all of the pleasure Mugsy gave me while I had her, and now I feel like I can give something back through Daisy. She is a wonderful, sweet, and loving dog, and is treasured by all of the students and staff. But best of all, I'm the lucky one who gets to take her home with me each night after work.❧

Ginny and Tiger

— Chapter Eight —

Hero Mutts

Thousands of lives in the United States and around the world are saved each year thanks to the heroic efforts of dogs. Time and again, dogs have proven their ability to sense danger and come to the rescue of their human companions, friends, neighbors, and often times other animals. The courageous mutts in this chapter have gone to great lengths to save lives, sometimes even risking their own in the process.

◆ ◆ ◆

Ginny
THE DOG WHO RESCUES CATS

The old saying "fighting like cats and dogs" is a foreign concept when it comes to Ginny. A terrier and husky mix who is unusually affectionate towards cats, Ginny and her human companion, Philip Gonzalez have helped rescue more than four hundred injured or abandoned cats during the past eight years. Ginny's incredible life story has been chronicled in two books: *The Dog Who Rescues Cats* and *The Blessing of the Animals*.

Like so many other mutts, Ginny started off in a cage at one of the country's five thousand animal shelters. She was found in an abandoned apartment building in Long Island, New York, left with her three puppies to starve to death. Along with her pups, Ginny was taken to a nearby animal shelter to be placed for adoption. Her pups were adopted within a few days, but mother Ginny still waited for a new home.

At the time, Philip was recovering from a terrible construction accident that had nearly cost him his right arm. His arm was saved, but he was unable to return to work. Philip's neighbor, Sheila, noticed that he had been very depressed since the accident and approached him with the idea of adopting a dog. At first Philip refused, but he eventually gave in, and agreed to go to the animal shelter with Sheila.

"I was sort of getting used to the idea of getting a dog, but I was thinking a big dog," explained Philip. "Maybe a German shepherd, an akita, a rottweiler, or a doberman pinscher. I thought only in terms of the dog being a purebred. I wanted a great-looking dog that other people would envy me for."

When Philip first spotted Ginny in her cage at the shelter, he mistook her for a German shepherd puppy. When he found out she was "nothing but a mutt," he immediately lost all interest. "She wasn't anything like the macho, purebred dog I'd already made my mind up to adopt," recalled Philip.

After a lot of coaxing from the shelter attendant and Sheila, Philip finally agreed to take Ginny out for a "test drive." By the time they came back from a short walk around the block, the two had already bonded. "Our eyes met, and when they did, I felt like a connection was being made," explained Philip. "I wasn't able to take my eyes off her, I could swear she smiled at me." He adopted Ginny that day and took her home.

It took Ginny some time to get adjusted to affection and food, since she'd had very little of both before Philip adopted her. The two began going for several walks a day around the neighborhood. Whenever Ginny saw a cat, she would pull hard on the leash, trying to get closer to it. Philip always held onto her tightly, fearing that she might go after one of the cats. One evening while out on a walk, Ginny began straining at her collar and whimpering incessantly. Philip accidentally dropped her leash, and before he could stop her, Ginny had run directly over to a stray cat. By the time Philip got there, Ginny was standing nose to nose with the cat, licking and grooming it. Philip was quite surprised, but relieved at the same time.

Philip and Ginny often went to visit her friends at the shelter from where she was adopted. Philip would barely make it through the shelter entrance when Ginny would pull him straight towards the cat room every time. On one visit she ran directly up to a cage with a white kitten inside, and began scratching at the cage and whimpering. Philip decided it was time to let Ginny have a cat of her own, so he adopted the kitten and named it Madam. A few weeks later, Philip discovered that Madam was completely deaf. It was as if Ginny had somehow sensed Madam's special needs, and wanted to care for her. Madam became the first on a long list of Ginny's cat rescues, most of which have been from the streets near Philip's home.

Ginny's feline friends include: Vogue, a homeless kitten she rescued from a group of cruel children who had been tossing her around like a football; Revlon, another cat she "found" at the shelter, who only had one eye; Bette Boop, a cat with no hind feet Ginny found at the vet's office; Topsy, a six-week old kitten Ginny found in an air-conditioning duct who was born with a brain disorder, and only able to roll around, not walk. And the list goes on and on.

"As long as there's a cat out there who needs extra love, a cat who has been abused, disabled or disfigured, a cat in trouble or in pain, Ginny somehow always finds them with her special radar," stated Philip. In fact she is so intent on finding and helping cats, that on a few occasions Ginny has risked her own life in the process. On one occasion, she pawed her way through a box filled with broken glass to rescue a kitten trapped at the bottom. Before Philip could stop her, Ginny's paws were badly grated from the incident.

Ten of "Ginny's cats," now live with her and Philip. Nightly, the two make their rounds, rain or shine, to deliver food to dozens of other abandoned cats in the neighborhood. Ginny has won numerous awards for her heroic acts including "The Humanitarian of the Year" from the Long Island Cat Fanciers Association.❖

Scotty
BEAM ME UP

In December 1997, a terrier mix named Scotty made national headlines when he helped rescue a twelve-year-old girl lost in a cold ravine near Little Rock, Arkansas. For twenty-four hours, he stayed by young Misty Harger's side, keeping her warm and alive in fourteen-degree weather.

The interesting thing about this story is that Scotty did not belong to Misty. He belonged to a local woman named Shirley Adams, who had adopted him from a shelter nearly eight years earlier. Misty was on an outing with her family when she became lost near the banks of the Buffalo River in Northwest Arkansas. Scotty happened upon her a few hours later and followed her as she walked deep into the cold river valley.

The local sheriff's department thought Misty had little chance of surviving the night in below-freezing temperatures. She was only wearing a light jacket and had removed her tennis shoes after they had gotten wet. A police helicopter with heat-seeking equipment was unable to locate her along the river nor could bloodhounds searching by ground. Searchers in a boat finally found Misty about a mile up the river from where she was last seen. She was found in the nick of time, just an hour and a half before a snow storm moved in.

Misty told the rescuers how Scotty had kept her awake throughout the night by barking incessantly at a white owl in a nearby tree. Scotty also had hidden her tennis shoes behind a rock after she removed them, which the rescuers said may have inadvertently saved her life. Without her shoes she couldn't wander around and perhaps fall into the freezing river.

Upon Scotty's return home he was treated to a hero's welcome and a special dinner. There was much discussion about whether the figure of a white owl Misty had seen was really an angel watching over her. There was no other explanation for her surviving the ordeal in such good shape, other than Scotty, who was named after the "Star Trek" character, and the famous line "Beam me up, Scotty❖"

Laurie Krenzel with Harley and Simon

Harley and Simon
A REASON TO LIVE
–Laurie Krenzel

My dogs, Harley and Simon, have never saved me from a burning building, or a specific life-threatening situation, but I credit them for my being the main reason I am here today to write this story.

As a child I was abused, and as a result developed critical anorexia nervosa and clinical depression in later years. I am five-feet, ten-inches tall, and at one point weighed only seventy-four pounds. I was so malnourished I could hardly walk. For the past nine years I have been recovering from both of these conditions. Although I credit much of my health to the kindness of strangers, friends and family, it was Harley and Simon who taught me how to love, laugh, and live again.

Simon had been abandoned at a grooming shop by his former owner who said he would have the dog destroyed if the groomer didn't take him. The groomer had to shave years of matting and dirt away just to decide what type of animal he was! Simon had been severely abused, and when I saw him cowering and shivering under the table I wondered what I was getting myself into. A friend drove us home that day with both of us sitting on opposite ends of the back seat, each contemplating the other. When I brought Simon into my apartment, I noticed how he hid behind my legs and shook—so afraid of everything. Through gentleness, lots of love and patience, Simon eventually came around. His transformation was amazing. Now he can't get enough of people and thinks everyone loves him.

When I adopted Simon I was working and going to college full time, and I was worried about him being too lonely during the day. I responded to an ad in the paper for a "schnoodle" (schnauzer and poodle mix), and that's how I adopted Harley.

From the minute he came home, Harley acted like he owned the place. He was quite the opposite of Simon. During the first few months of Harley's reign I thought Simon was going to have a nervous breakdown. I don't know what happened to change their relationship, but Harley taught Simon how to play and bark again, and they became best of buddies. Before Harley came along, Simon rarely ever played with his toys. Harley on the other hand, loves his toys and knows each one by name. He would run after Simon with a favorite soft toy and bop him on the head with it until he would give in and play.

I saw a lot of Simon in myself. Like me, he was abused and afraid of people and the outside world. Watching the effects that Harley had on him, and the amazing transformation he went through, gave me the inspiration to go on. I saw through Simon's eyes that with a lot of love and patience, life is definitely worth living. A lot of people might think of Harley and Simon as just two little mutts, but to me they are the lights of my life. They are without a doubt my heroes! ❧

Buck

TO CATCH A THIEF

Petopia and Rescue Program, a dog rescue group in New York, was collecting donations for its cause one evening in Greenwich Village. They had set up a booth on the street corner, and were busy talking with people and taking donations, when a man walked up acting like he was about to put a dollar in the jar. Instead, he grabbed all of their money and ran off. When the thief vanished into the crowd, the group's volunteers moved across the street where they thought it would be safer. But just a half-hour later, the man returned again and snatched more money from the jar.

One of the rescue dogs they had with them, a lab mix named Buck, sprang into action, chasing and tackling the thug, forcing him to drop the fistful of cash. The money went flying everywhere, and several people helped pick it up and return it. But unfortunately, the thief managed to escape. "Buck was just wonderful. He knew this man had done something wrong, ran after him and pushed him down," recalled Petopia board member, Lonnie Jackson.

Buck really saved the day, and as a result he saved himself. After a story of Buck's heroic deed appeared in the newspaper the following day, Petopia was flooded with calls from people who wanted to adopt him. A few days later he went home with a new family.❖

Hero Mutt "Hall of Fame"

Since 1944, Ken-L-Ration Dog Food Company has presented the annual "Dog Hero of the Year" award to dogs who have demonstrated extraordinary courage and bravery in attempts to save the lives of people or animals. To date, a total of thirteen winners have been mutts, and dozens of other mutts have been awarded as runner-ups. The following mutts are past recipients of the coveted Dog Hero Award.

Lady and Tommy Abel

Heinz Pet Products

Lady—1959
Mehlville, Montana

The first mutt to receive the Ken-L-Ration Dog Hero award was a collie mix named Lady. She saved the life of a three-year old family member, Tommy Abel, who had become stuck in a clay-mud swamp after wandering away from home. Lady had accompanied Tommy on his walk that day, and immediately went to get help when she realized he was in trouble.

Lady took off, running through nearby woods, barking at the top of her lungs to summon help. Two telephone repair workers followed Lady for several miles through the woods until they reached an exhausted, cold, and very frightened Tommy. After several attempts to free Tommy from the swamp, they finally succeeded. The workers returned Tommy to his parents with a very proud Lady in tow.❖

 Patches–1965
Spanaway, Washington

A terrier mix named Patches towed his owner to the dock after he had slipped on the pier, injuring his legs, and falling into an icy lake. Then, while he tried to climb out of the lake, he fainted and fell in again. Once more, Patches pulled him to safety❧

Ringo–1968
Euless, Texas

A half-hour before two-year old Randy Saleh's parents had scheduled to have a gate installed around their home to keep him from wandering, he had gone off unnoticed. Fortunately Randy's dog, Ringo, had followed him. When Randy decided it would be fun to play in the middle of a busy intersection, Ringo sprang into action, barking and running circles around the boy to divert oncoming cars until rescuers arrived❧

Ringo and Randy Saleh

Heinz Pet Products

Ricky Sherry and Trixie

Trixie-1971
Lynn, Massachusetts

Trixie used extraordinary intelligence to save two-year old family member, Ricky Sherry, after the child had tumbled into an icy pond near his home. The boy somehow managed to squirm through an opening in the backyard fence and Trixie hastened to follow him. Less than fifteen minutes later, Ricky lost his footing on a nearby bank, and fell into the frigid pond below. Trixie dove into the freezing water to try and retrieve the little boy, but to no avail.

Trixie then dragged herself out of the pond, and ran off to find help. The first person Trixie encountered was a neighbor. She saw right away that something was wrong and followed Trixie to the pond. She jumped into the water and pulled the boy out, and then ran to call paramedics. Luckily Ricky survived the ordeal, and even though he was just two, he seemed to really understand that Trixie saved his life❖

Donald Essig and Skippy

Skippy–1974
Santa Ana, California

Skippy placed himself between an eighteen-inch rattlesnake and five-year old Donald Essig, as the snake was poising to strike. While saving the boy's life, the brave collie mix incurred the snake's bite, and ended up in intensive care for three days at the animal hospital. Skippy made a complete recovery and came home to a most grateful little boy and his family❖

Zorro–1976
Orangevale, California

While on a hiking trip, Zorro's owner fell eighty-five feet into a rocky river. The shepherd mix immediately sprang into action, and bolted down the mountain to pull his owner ashore. Zorro remained by his side until a rescue team arrived. Rescuers said that the man surely would have perished if the dog had not pulled him from the treacherous river❖

Woodie-1980
Cleveland, Ohio

Rae Anne Knitter and her fiance, Ray Thomas, were taking a walk with their dog, Woodie along a nature trail. Ray, an amateur photographer, wanted to capture the spectacular view from atop a steep shale cliff. He lost his footing and fell eighty feet, ending up face-down and unconscious in the stream below.

Without hesitation, Woodie dove off the cliff to help Ray. She broke both hips in the fall, but still struggled to nudge Ray's face to keep it out of the water. When rescuers reached the injured pair, they agreed that if it wasn't for Woodie, Ray would probably have drowned. Both Ray and Woodie fully recovered❖

King-1981
Granite Falls, Washington

The Carlson family was fast asleep when a fire broke out in their utility room the day after Christmas. Their dog, a shepherd mix named King, was sleeping in the adjoining family room. Instead of making a speedy exit through the sliding glass doors that were left open for him, King fought his way into the fire. He clawed and chewed until he was able to get through the plywood door that barred him from the utility room.

He charged through the burning room into the bedroom where sixteen-year old Pearl was sleeping. He whined and nudged her until she awoke, then they both rushed to her parents' bedroom to alert them to the fire. The home was completely destroyed, but thanks to King, everyone escaped. King suffered badly burned paws, a gash on his back, and a mouthful of splinters from the ordeal❖

Tango–1985
Port Townsend, Washington

Tango, an Australian shepherd and border collie mix, saved his owner, Al Choate, when he intercepted the brutal attack of an angry cow. When the cow began attacking Al, Tango jumped up and bit into the cow's lip and held on so Al could get away. Tango escaped unharmed, although Al suffered fractured ribs and other internal injuries from the incident❧

Tango and Al Choate

Harvey Schmidt, Champ, and Buddy

Champ, Buddy–1986
Granite Falls, Washington

Champ and Buddy saved the life of truck driver, Marvin Dacar, who become trapped beneath a 2,600-pound tractor that had fallen on his foot. The dogs led their owners, Harvey and Annelies Schmidt, to the deserted warehouse where Marvin lay bleeding profusely. Doctors said that he would have surely died from shock and loss of blood if Champ and Buddy hadn't found him and gone for help❧

Lera Stein and Buppy

BUPPY-1988
Tulsa, Oklahoma

Adam and Burr Emrick were visiting their disabled grandmother, Lera Stein, after school when a fire broke out in her house. The boys' collie mix, Buppy, immediately ran to alert them to ensure their safe escape, and to help their grandmother out of the house. Although Buppy's nose was burned, and his coat singed by flames, he would not leave the burning front porch until he saw the boy's grandmother standing safely by the side of the road❧

Sheena-1991
St. Petersburg, Florida

Sheena and John Rayner

Sheena, a shepherd mix, tied with a weimaraner named Willy for first place as Dog Hero of the Year in 1991. The daring Sheena rescued her disabled companion, John Rayner, during an attempted robbery assault in a supermarket parking lot. John was about to put groceries in his car when two men attacked him from behind. The assailants began to scuffle with John, demanding his watch and wallet, while Sheena watched frantically from inside the car. When

John finally managed to pull open the car door, Sheena, who he described as "normally loving and maternal," bared her teeth and lunged at the assailants. With one attacker on the ground, Sheena chased the other for several blocks as he fled the scene. Ironically, only six months earlier, John had saved Sheena's life when he discovered her lying unconscious and badly cut in his yard☙

Bailey–1996
Newport, Kentucky

Bailey and Chester Jenkins

This courageous Chesapeake retriever and lab mix fought off a two thousand-pound Belgian blue bull to save the life of his owner, Chester Jenkins. Chester had turned his back to the bull for only a second, when the angry animal charged and tossed him several yards into a watering trough. The bull then pinned him between the trough and the fence and raked his sharp hooves, about the size of bowling balls, repeatedly across Chester's back.

Bailey heard the commotion and came running. Without a moment's hesitation, he went right for the bull's head, grabbing onto its nose and ears with his teeth. Despite the bull's efforts to throw Bailey off, the attack gave Chester time to squirm under the fence to safety.

Bailey then retreated from the bull and took off for the house to get help. When he wasn't able to find Chester's wife, Iris, he ran back to Chester to help him get up to the house. Bailey was unharmed, but Chester suffered crushed ribs, a broken shoulder, and a punctured lung. After a long recuperation, Chester was able to return to his work as a farmer. Bailey's heroics made headline news around the country☙

Gus

CHAPTER NINE

Magnificent Mutts Across America

When I first began working on this book in early 1995, I sent an announcement to newspapers calling for photo and story submissions. Nearly two thousand people throughout the United States responded to the call for submissions. I was absolutely amazed! I knew there were a lot of mutt lovers out there, but this was more of a response than I had ever dreamed of. Each day, my mail box was like a treasure trove. I couldn't wait to read all of the stories, and see the photos of so many wonderful mutts and their people from coast to coast. The following stories were culled from these submissions.

◆ ◆ ◆

GUS

DETERMINED TO STAY
—Sharon Russick, Florida

One day, a stray dog collapsed in front of my barn suffering from malnutrition and a beating so severe he could barely walk. My initial attempts to approach him were unsuccessful. He displayed an intense fear of people, obviously the result of prior abusive treatment.

He must have sensed my good intentions, as he slowly began accepting my offerings of food and affection. I cared for him and named him Gus. His transformation in appearance and personality were truly remarkable. From what was once a pathetic, abused dog, emerged a handsome, personable individual who happily greeted customers and visitors at my farm. He became my inseparable companion, even trotting beside me when I rode my horse.

Our life together was soon disrupted, and Gus was moved to another farm located fifteen miles away. He refused to accept the separation, and kept running back to my farm. His treacherous trips involved traveling along the busy Florida Turnpike and swimming across alligator-infested canals.

Gus made a total of five trips back. Each time he would walk into my barn, wagging his tail furiously in the excitement of being reunited with me. It was finally decided that Gus and I should remain together. He is sitting beside me as I write this❧

Trouble

TRUE TO THE END

For seventy-eight year old Bill Drifmeyer, seeing his dog, Trouble, made life worth living. So much so, that he didn't mind paying the $42 round-trip taxi fare for Trouble to come and visit him at the hospice care home.

A few times a week, Bill sent a cab to pick up Trouble at his ex-wife Edna's house and bring him to the Hospice House Woodside in Largo, Florida. "I'll never forget the first taxi driver that came to pick up Trouble. I opened the door, and handed him the leash and said 'Here he is,' and the guy thought it was some kind of practical joke," recalled Edna, who was temporarily caring for Trouble. "That was the first time he'd ever had a dog as a single passenger."

Each time Bill sent for Trouble, he would wait outside the hospice entrance anxiously pacing back and forth. "The minute Bill saw the taxi

Photo by Scott Keeler © St. Petersburg Times

Bill Drifmeyer and Trouble

pull up with Trouble inside, his expression would immediately change. He was always so happy to see his dog," explained Bill's hospice counselor, Peter Coburn.

Normally dogs aren't allowed overnight at the hospice, but Bill was in failing health due to cancer, and the staff knew how much it meant to him to be with his dog. They made an exception and allowed Trouble to live in Bill's room. At first Trouble was no problem. He slept on the bed next to Bill, and accompanied him on daily walks around the grounds. But Trouble started becoming overly protective of Bill, sometimes growling at the nurses. And he would startle and scare Bill's roommate with his loud, unexpected barks.

After a few weeks of trouble with Trouble, the staff informed Bill that his dog would have to leave. So off went Trouble in a cab back to Edna's house. Five days went by and Bill couldn't bear the separation any longer. He secretly called for a cab to pick up Trouble and bring him to the hospice. The two were quite happy to see each other, but the staff wasn't too amused. They allowed Bill to spend a few hours with Trouble, and then put the dog back in the cab to Edna's house after rounding up money for his fare.

After that incident, Bill's health failed further. Trouble was the only family member or friend who had come to visit him at the hospice in a few months. Edna was not in good health herself and it was difficult for her to get there, and Bill's children lived out of the area.

About a month later, a cab pulled up to the hospice driveway with guess who inside—Trouble. The hospice staff threw up their hands and moved Bill and Trouble into a private room until they could come up with another solution.

When word of Bill's plight got out, the nearby Advantage Pet Center called to offer assistance. They kindly offered to provide free room and board for Trouble for as long as necessary so he could be closer to Bill. Bill's counselor, Peter, picked up the dog each morning, brought him to the hospice to spend the day with Bill, then took him back to the Pet Center at night. This was a happy compromise for everyone.

"Trouble always knew exactly where to go," explained Peter. "As soon as we walked in the hospice entrance, he'd head right for Bill's room and jump on the bed. He was a very active dog, but when it came to Bill he was always calm and gentle. I think he sensed that Bill was very sick." All of the staff loved Trouble, and sometimes they would give in and let Bill keep him overnight.

Bill was growing concerned about what would happen to his beloved dog after he died. He wanted to find a loving home for Trouble before it was too late, fearing that he might end up in the wrong hands. He spoke with Peter and other hospice staff about his concern for Trouble. Word got out about Bill's concern for Trouble, and local newspapers ran a story hoping to help find a new home for his dog. The hospice was flooded with calls from people wanting to adopt Trouble.

"It made Bill very happy to know that so many people were concerned about Trouble," said Peter. The hospice agreed to arrange meetings for Bill with prospective adopters. He hoped to find a retiree to take in Trouble, preferably with a taste for Southern cooking. "He likes corn bread and beans—he's a country boy," Bill said in a newspaper interview.

Edna saw how concerned Bill was about Trouble's future, and volunteered to take the dog back to live with her permanently. Over the next few months she took Trouble to visit Bill on several occasions. On a Thursday in December was the last time Edna and Trouble would see Bill—he died that Saturday. "That dog meant everything to him. At least he went with some peace of mind, knowing that Trouble would be in good hands," stated Peter.

Since Bill's passing, Edna and Trouble have become great friends, but it's apparent that he still misses Bill. "If I let him out of the house now, I'm sure he'd find his way right back to the Hospice House to look for Bill. I know he really misses him a lot," lamented Edna ♣

⌐◦ ⌐◦ ⌐◦

"The one absolutely unselfish friend that man can have in this selfish world, the one that never deserts him, the one that never proves ungrateful or treacherous, is his dog."

GEORGE GRAHAM VEST

Helene Gorman and Lizbeth

Lizbeth

A TREASURED COMPANION

—Helene Gorman, New York

I am eighty years old and the very lucky companion of my lovely Lizbeth. When I went to adopt a dog at the local animal shelter, I saw Liz and thought she had the sweetest face in the world.

She goes everywhere with me, and my entire neighborhood, including bank tellers and store clerks, know her by name. I often wonder who would give up a dog as wonderful as Liz, however their loss is definitely my gain. My life would be very different without the pleasure of her company❖

Photo © Kelly K. McFaul Solem

Kacey lives in Minnesota with the Barleu family.

Kacey

⚬ ⚬ ⚬

"Through the eyes of a dog, all people are beautiful
—unfortunately it's not always a two-way street."

ANONYMOUS

Rosemary Calhoun

Kelli O'Rear and Rusty

Rusty

OLD DOGS NEED LOVE TOO

Day after day, for nearly ten years, Rusty waited with a hopeful look in his eyes each time someone approached his cage at the shelter. He was getting old, almost sixteen. His rust-colored coat had become dull and arthritis was beginning to take its toll. The chances of someone adopting a dog that age are pretty slim, but the Animal Protection League in South Carolina is a no-kill shelter, so Rusty was welcome to live out the rest of his life there.

For the past three years, eight-year old Kelli O'Rear had been volunteering at the shelter, helping to feed and groom the dogs. Her mother, Bobbi, is the shelter manager, and each day after school Kelli worked at the shelter caring for all the dogs.

Bobbi noticed that Kelli was taking a special liking to Rusty. "She would sit and talk to him, gently patting and brushing his coat, or sometimes pull out a stethoscope from her little 'doctor's bag' to listen to his heart. Some days, she would bring in a bag packed with brushes, toenail clippers, baby wipes, and perfume to pamper Rusty," recalled Bobbi. Kelli prepared Rusty's food (special gourmet meals) each day that she was there, and then in advance when she wasn't there so she knew Rusty was getting a nutritious diet.

One day, while Bobbi was cleaning out one of the dog's cages, she turned to see Kelli kneeling at Rusty's pen with her head down, sobbing. "When I asked her what was wrong, I had to hold back the tears myself. She told me that she didn't want Rusty to die in the shelter without first having a home and a family that loved him," Bobbi explained. So it was decided that Rusty would finally have a place to call home. A place where he could live out his remaining years basking in the love of this caring little girl. Needless to say, Kelli was thrilled.

After six months in his new home, Rusty's once sad eyes now gleamed with happiness. Rusty's companion, Kelli, is a young spirit who is wise far beyond her eight years, and she is determined to make this world a better place for dogs like Rusty.

Kelli described her very best friend this way: "Rusty is such a wise old fellow. He reminds me of my grandfather who is gentle and kind to me. When I'm talking to Rusty and he is looking at me with his big brown eyes, I think I can see all the way down deep into his heart where he keeps all of his feelings and love. Sometimes he seems sad, but I think that's because he knows he'll never be young again, or maybe he's just tired. Spending time with Rusty makes me feel safe and happy, just like when I sit in my grandfather's lap. Old dogs like Rusty just want to be close to the people they love❧"

Shortly before this book went to press, Rusty had a severe stroke. Kelli was with Rusty to the very end, cradling his head in her lap as her mom drove them to the vet where he was euthanized.

Photo © Susan Peacock, S. Downing Photography

Edens Houston and Smidge from Houston, Texas

Smidge

❖ ❖ ❖

"I'd rather have inches of dog than miles of pedigree."

Dana Burnett

Mort

A PRICELESS FRIEND

—Kelly Setlock, Pennsylvania

All I ever had growing up were purebred dogs, and now that I have a mutt, I see such a difference. In my opinion, most purebreds, such as my parents' two lhaso apsos, are especially spoiled. They're used to always having the good life, and don't know what it's like to be down and out, alone and abandoned. Like most adopted mutts, Mort knows what it's like to have it bad, and now that she has it good, she's eternally grateful.

Mort is a big hit in our neighborhood. When she looks at people and smiles with her silly little crooked mouth, they can't help but smile back. She has a pretty bad underbite.

Mort is my little buddy and goes everywhere with me. She's even got her own life preserver for when we go out boating. She loves boating and many other activities. Who would have ever expected this little dog who was abandoned on the "Burma road" in St. Clair, Pennsylvania, would end up living the good life. I paid a $30 fee to adopt her—so inexpensive a price for such a priceless friend, my mutt, Mort.

Sharon Deanne

Flynn
MEDICAL MIRACLE MUTT
—Sharon Deanne, Texas

Found abandoned by a drainage ditch at just six weeks old, Flynn had quite a rough start in life. From the beginning Flynn demonstrated amazing courage and a strong will to live. At two years of age, he displayed an even more incredible will to survive.

It was a few days before Christmas in 1991, and I was busy taking care of some last-minute holiday details. When I stopped for a break, I didn't see Flynn anywhere. He's usually always right by my side. Immediately I broke into a panic, searching frantically all over the house and yard. All of the sudden, I remembered that some repairmen were just at the house. My worst fears came true—they had accidentally left the gate open, and Flynn had gotten out.

I ran outside, yelling his name everywhere. When I got a few blocks away, I noticed something laying in the middle of the road up ahead. As I got closer, I cringed in horror. It was Flynn, laying in shock and covered in blood. He's only about fifteen pounds and apparently he had been viciously attacked by a large chow.

Luckily I had my cell phone in hand, and called the vet, who instructed, "Don't move him, I'll be right there, I'm on my way." Within minutes he arrived, and took Flynn and me back to his hospital. He worked on Flynn late into the night, and then transported him to a surgical specialist. Flynn's back had been broken. My husband and I told the vet that if there was any hope of saving Flynn, to please go ahead and operate.

The next day, Christmas Eve, the vet told us that Flynn would live, but there was very little hope of him ever using his back legs again. Most likely Flynn wouldn't be able to perform his bodily functions without our assistance. We would have to manually express his bladder and bowels two to three times a day. A few days later Flynn came home, and for the next several weeks we cared for him around the clock.

About two months later, I was outside doing some yard work, when to my utter amazement, Flynn dragged himself outside through the doggie door. It scared and shocked me, but then I realized he would fight to get better no matter what.

Today, Flynn can not only walk on all four legs, but he can run up and down the length of our fence in the yard. Sometimes he even jumps up to try and catch a bird in flight. He has also regained some nerve rejuvenation in his lower back, which gives us all hope that one day he may be able to perform his daily functions all by himself.

Both of the vets who worked to save Flynn's life are amazed by his incredible recovery. They say Flynn is truly a little miracle dog. Flynn has been a great inspiration to us and has taught us how very precious life is ❧

Photo © Gregg A. Thompson

Joanne Dickson and her dogs, Meisha and Margo, enjoy rollerblading in St. Cloud, Minnesota.

meisha and margo

Maranda
THE POWER OF LOVE
—Kendra Walker, Tennessee

If you have ever suffered in life and felt like giving up, I wish you could meet my dog, Maranda. If she could talk, she would tell you a wonderful story about how she survived abuse and neglect to come to a loving home.

In the summer of 1991, I was devastated when my dog vanished from my backyard. After a month of daily visits to the shelter, and scouring the neighborhood, there was still no sign of her. On my last visit to the shelter, I spotted a shy blonde puppy, and knew I wouldn't sleep that night unless I took her home with me. I named her Maranda.

Sadly, Maranda had been badly beaten by her previous owners and was in need of medical attention. She was also terribly fearful of men. Never knowing what it was like to be loved, she had a difficult time accepting love and affection at her new home.

I spent many hours and days working with Maranda, trying to help her overcome her shyness and fearfulness. After a few months, there was still very little change, and my boyfriend was losing hope of Maranda ever becoming a lovable dog. He agreed to give her one more week, and if there was still no change, we would have to find her another home.

That week I worked day and night, trying to generate a positive response from Maranda. I prayed for an answer to how I could help her heal and become more trusting. On the very last day of that week, my prayers were answered. That morning, I was taken by surprise when Maranda came bouncing over to me, and showered me with kisses—that was the first time she had really shown any affection.

From that point on, Maranda's transformation was remarkable. She blossomed into the most wonderful, loving dog. Maranda taught us that no matter how much we suffer in life, we can overcome almost anything with a little love, and a lot of faith from someone who cares❖

Ogden

THE AQUABEAST

—In Ogden's words as told to: Rebecca Carley, New York

Hi, my name is Odgen, although my friends all call me "Aquabeast" because I just love the water! As far as anyone can tell, I have some German shepherd and some type of spaniel blood coursing through my veins. I'm not sure exactly how old I am, but I adopted my human mom a little over seven years ago. Well, anyway, here's my story:

My previous owner had treated me badly and removed my tail, so I decided to hit the road. After looking for a safe place to lay my weary head and very large ears, I ended up at the entrance to a hospital where my "mom" was a surgeon at the time.

Rebecca Carley

Ogden

Even though I was covered from head to toe with grease and dirt, I made many friends who worked at the hospital and would often share their meals with me. I was quite content, but wanted more than anything a home to call my own. Who would I choose to share my life with?

One of the many people who fed me every day was a lady they called Dr. Becky. She had brown eyes just like me, and always stopped to give me a bite to eat and pat my dirty head. I could smell the scent of many other dogs on her, so I knew I'd really have to turn the charm on to get her to take me home. I used what I call my "extra slo-mo" technique—a long, slow lick which I would plant on her feet and legs whenever I saw her.

It worked! One day she pulled her car up next to my hang out, and said "let's go home," and I jumped right in. Well, that's the happy end of my tale (no pun intended, since I don't have one)✿

Zsasu is the companion of Joyce Anderson of Tennessee.

ZSGSU

❧ ❧ ❧

"No one appreciates the very special genius of your conversation as a dog does."

CHRISTOPHER MORLEY

Kathyrn Wilson

Tiano

MY LITTLE SATO

–Kathryn Wilson, Georgia

When people first enter my home, they are greeted by a solid black, skinny, spindly legged creature, who has sometimes been mistaken for a long-legged rat. Everyone always asks me, "What kind of dog is that?" and I reply, "A Puerto Rican sato," which is the Spanish word for mutt. However, my English-speaking friends do not know this, so they think he is a rare breed of some sort.

I found Tiano in June 1994 while driving along a highway in Puerto Rico. I was on my way back from touring a Tiano Indian Reservation, and stopped by the side of the road to admire the beautiful ocean view. Suddenly, I saw a tiny black bundle no bigger than my hand, crouched in a pothole, quivering and scared. Upon closer examination, I realized it was a stray puppy. Although I'd seen many strays in Puerto Rico since moving there a few weeks earlier, I couldn't resist the urge to help this one. Like me, he had been surviving on his own after being thrown into a foreign world of harsh reality.

I took him home and named him Tiano, after the Indian Reservation I had just visited. Our first stop was the local vet, where he was given vaccines and treated for anemia and hundreds of ant bites on his stomach from lying in the streets.

Tiano proved to be an eager-to-please pup. He was house trained in no time, and when I told him it was time to go to sleep, he would take his baby pacifier (which he found and adopted himself), and curl up in his own little bed. Before long I found myself relying on Tiano for companionship. He was the only friend I had in my new Puerto Rican surroundings, and to whom I could come home from work and speak my native language, English. Tiano later became bilingual, learning commands in both Spanish and English.

Now that Tiano is full grown he is unique indeed, in both looks and personality. His tastes are particular, for he insists on watching the sunset every evening, and will *only* eat his food if I am brushing my teeth at the time. He likes to lounge on my down pillow, his lanky legs folded up several times in a neat, black package, resembling a large tea bag. He also plays hide-and-seek with me, and I've only been able to outsmart him one time when I hid on a shelf in my closet with the door closed for twenty minutes!

Tiano never lets me out of his sight for a moment. Whenever I'm working, he jumps up in my lap and curls up until I'm finished. The best time with Tiano is at the end of each day. We cuddle up together in my bed, and I disclose my feelings, discuss my thoughts, and depict my ideas as I stroke his belly until we both fall asleep spoon-fashion❖

Animal Friends

Harry

THE LOUDEST AND SCRUFFIEST

—Alma Wisniewski, Pennsylvania

When people ask me where I found Harry, I tell them that he found me. He yelped the loudest and looked the scruffiest when I went to the animal shelter to look for a dog. When I took him out to the play yard, he landed his front paws right in my lap and gave me this soulful gaze, that made the rest history.

© Three Dog Bakery

Sarah Jean
The Biscuit Queen

A lab mix named Sarah Jean is one of three canine co-founders of the Three Dog Bakery in Kansas City, Missouri. As described by owners, Mark Beckloff and Dan Dye, the bakery is "a Canine Confectionery, a Pooch Patisserie, and a Mecca for Mutts." Their first bakery was so successful that a mail-order business was started and other bakeries have been opened in cities across the United States.

Mark and Dan adopted Sarah Jean more than eight years ago from an area animal shelter. Sarah and her "sisters," Dottie the dalmatian, and Gracie the great dane, have the fun job of taste-testing all of the goodies that are baked up. A handsome portrait of the three sisters adorns the walls of each bakery.

Sarah Jean kindly donated two of her favorite recipes for the book: Banana Mutt Cookies and Mutt Muffins.❖

❧ BANANA MUTT COOKIES ❧

3 cups bananas, mashed

1 teaspoon vanilla

6 cups oats

1 cup peanuts, chopped

1/3 cup applesauce, unsweetened

Preheat oven to 350 degrees:
Mix all ingredients together thoroughly. Use teaspoon to drop on baking sheet sprayed with a nonstick cooking spray and press flat. Bake for approximately 15 minutes, or until slightly brown. Cool on cooling rack, then store in airtight container. Yield: approximately two dozen cookies.

❧ MUTT MUFFINS ❧

1 apple

2 carrots

2 tablespoons honey

2 3/4 cups water

1/4 teaspoon vanilla

1 egg

In food processor puree the apple. Shred carrot with hand shredder. In a bowl mix all wet ingredients together and add pureed apple. Mix wet ingredients thoroughly.

4 cups whole wheat flour

1/2 cup raisins

1 tablespoon baking powder

1 tablespoon cinnamon

1 tablespoon nutmeg

Combine dry ingredients. Add wet ingredients to dry and mix thoroughly, making sure none of dry mixture is left. With an ice cream scoop, fill a muffin pan 3/4 full, sprayed with nonstick spray. Bake at 350 degrees for approximately 1 hour. Yield: 12 to 14 muffins.

Recipes © Three Dog Bakery, reprinted with permission

Doug Hocking

Alley

GETTING UP IN EARS

–Ellen Reinhardt, California

When we first found Alley, we thought she was just a puppy that would grow into her huge ears, which, as you can see, are quite over-sized for her face. After taking her to the vet, we were surprised to find out that she was already full grown. We think she is part Basenji and part something else—the something else is the part that barks❖

Debbie Bailey

Clementine

A REAL TROOPER

–Debbie Bailey, Georgia

I went to the humane society with a friend. She was supposed to get a dog, not me! I had a seventeen-year old poodle at home—I didn't need a dog. I walked through the door of the shelter and there she was, making a huge fuss to get my attention. I got her out of the cage, put her to my chest, and she immediately got quiet and buried her head. She went home with me and I named her Clementine.

In the early years Clementine was a terror. Now when I look back, some of the things that she did were pretty funny. But there's also a sad part to Clementine's story. Last November, she began steadily losing weight and throwing up continuously. She was diagnosed with a condition called megaesophagus, which causes deterioration of the muscles in the esophagus. It usually only happens with puppies, and is often fatal. Clementine was nine and the prognosis was poor. She stayed at the vet hospital for weeks on oxygen and IV fluids, while they figured out what could be done for her.

Given her age and the outlook, they suggested putting her to sleep. The doctor told me that as an alternative we could try feeding her through a tube in her side. He warned me that it would be very time consuming, and he wasn't sure what quality of life she would have. After carefully weighing the situation, I decided to take Clementine home.

Pneumonia was a major risk, due to the aspiration of her saliva. She could take nothing by mouth, and spit up saliva a few times a day. So far we've battled pneumonia three times. I puree her food with water to make a thick liquid, then use small syringes to pump it through the tube in her side. I have to go very slowly in order to avoid causing her stomach to cramp. It takes an hour in the morning, and an hour at night to feed her. She lays between my legs very quietly on the floor. When the timer goes off, she knows we're done. She gets up, stretches, and turns to give me a kiss. It's all worth it.

It's been a year now, and Clementine is still very active and loves to play ball. Although her esophagus is still not functioning, I'd say her life is at about 80 percent of what it used to be. Her doctor told me that I "loved her back to health❧"

Clementine died in May 1996.

Meredith Smith and Sparky

Sparky

A MUTT OF ALL TRADES

—In Sparky's words as told to: The Smiths, Tennessee

Yo, Sparky Smith here! My family has put together a list of my likely heritage for your book, so here goes: Blue tick hound (I'm a Tennessee boy, love to howl, sniff out squirrels and possums, and point when I feel like it); bulldog (got a mean underbite, and very tenacious); Jack Russell terrier (I can leap tall sofas in a single bound); rottweiler (don't come in my backyard without an invitation); and last but not least, golden retriever (I'm loyal to death, and nothing matters to me but my kids Alex and Meredith).

Normally I don't go for social climbing and getting my handsome snout in some fancy mutt book, but I wanted to show off to my best pal, Faline, a corgi who's always looking down her well-bred nose at me. Man, I can't wait to stick her nose in this! ❧

Norm Anderson

Barney

Barney

A GOOD OMEN

—Norm Anderson, Iowa

In July 1990, Barney adopted us. It was a Saturday, and we were preparing to go out for a round of golf. As we were loading our equipment in the van, my wife, Becky, reached down for her golf shoes, and jumped about ten feet. There lying in the shadows of the garage was a very sickly looking puppy. He had a pronounced sore on his ears from fly bites, and was surely starving. We gave him water, and borrowed dog food from our neighbor, which the hungry pup quickly devoured.

After some discussion, we felt this must be an omen that we should have a dog. We wanted to make sure that he didn't belong to someone, so we took him to the local humane society. After a week, no one came forward to claim him, and Barney became the newest member of our family.He grew to be quite a large dog, weighing in at seventy-five pounds, but every pound of him is pure love.

Barney is loved by the neighborhood kids who all know him by name. He loves to go everywhere with us, and especially enjoys visiting our parents' homes. Barney doesn't like to sleep on our bed, but for some reason he insists on sharing the hide-a-bed with us at our parents' homes. Picture two adults with a seventy-five pound dog, his legs fully extended, in a small hide-a-bed. It's like something you'd see on "America's Funniest Home Videos."

We're forever grateful that Barney chose our garage when he was hungry and scared those eight years ago. We can't imagine our life without him.❧

Lucky

MYSTERY MUTT

—*Jodi Rogala, Pennsylvania*

Lucky has a nick name, "Rat Dog," because she truly looks like one. I like to tell people that she is a science experiment gone wrong, really wrong. She definitely has a face that only a mother could love. We don't know from what blended heritage she came, but we love her more than anything.

Photo © Tere E. Ireys, Benjemax Studios

Harold and Michelle Naylor

Harold

THE MOST ADORABLE UGLIEST DOG

—Michelle Naylor, Arizona

About three years ago, my sister called to tell me about a dog she had just found wandering the streets. She said he was "the ugliest dog ever," and that I had to come over and see him right away. At the time, she was in the middle of a divorce, and I wasn't really in the mood to drive over to her ex's house to see an ugly dog. But something compelled me to go.

Ugly? He was adorable, a face full of personality. I fell in love immediately, and since my sister was trying to find him a home, I took him. I named him Harold, and he became the third canine member of our family.

Harold is between twelve and fourteen years old. He sleeps a lot, but never past dinner. Dinner time is always a celebration for him. He springs from his bed, spinning and jumping, whirling like a dervish, and barking like a fiend. Harold's credo is "To eat is to live, to live is to eat." One time I came home to find him stuck in the cat door that leads to the basement, trying to reach for a bowl of cat food. It was quite a funny sight.

A few weeks later, I came home from work, and noticed that Harold seemed abnormally chubby. Worried about what he could have gotten into, I rushed him to the pet emergency clinic. X-rays showed he was absolutely packed with food—so full he couldn't pass it through. They pumped his stomach to the tune of $200.

Later that evening I discovered that "someone" had gotten into the basement and pulled a twenty-pound bag of cat food off the shelf and consumed a good portion of it. Harold only weighs thirteen pounds and is just over a foot tall, so you can imagine my horror. We rigged the cat door the next day so he couldn't get through anymore. He wasn't too pleased about that.

Harold is, without a doubt, the funniest dog we've ever known. Not a day goes by where I haven't laughed out loud at his antics. I never knew such a tiny creature could bring such joy and laughter to a family. We gave Harold a home, but he has repaid us many times over by giving us the gift of himself. By the way, my sister now thinks Harold is the "cutest dog ever!" ❧

Maray Ayres

Zoshie is the companion of Maray Ayres of Southern California.

Zoshie

❧ A STARTLING STATISTIC ❧

In just six years, one unspayed female dog and her unspayed or unneutered offspring can produce up to 67,000 puppies.

Photo © Karryn

Sam and Sadie

FRIENDS FOR LIFE

—In Sadie's words as told to: Sharon Surber, California

On a sunny day in Southern California, a little mutt named Sadie roamed the city streets. She had been on the streets for a couple of days and had but a few thoughts in mind—food, water, a warm bed, and lots of love. Well, I'll let her tell the rest of the story, since she's the one who really knows it best:

Here comes a pretty lady in a neat looking truck. Maybe she'll give me a ride to her house where I'll get lots of food and love. The lady picked me up and put me in her truck. Sitting next to me was the funniest looking dog I'd ever seen. She claimed to be a lhasa and poodle mix, but she had the longest body and the shortest legs. She said her name was Sam. I could tell she seemed a little nervous, and perhaps sensed trouble.

When the truck pulled up at our new home, I heard many of my own kind talking. Some sounded sorrowful and some very scared. What is this place where the truck has taken us? The sign on the front of the building read "Animal Shelter." The truck lady took me and Sam inside, and put us in kennels side by side. They gave us some food and water. I curled up next to the wire fence and Sam curled up next to me. We kept each other warm and secure.

As days passed, a few of our friends were taken out the back door for walks, but never seemed to return. We wondered where they had gone! People came in the front door, sometimes walking briskly up and down the aisles. They seemed to be looking for something specific, I'm not sure what. On this particular day, a nice looking couple came by my cage and stopped for awhile. The man shook his head and walked on, but the woman stayed a while looking at me. Oh, I almost forgot, my name is Sadie. I tried to look cute, but I really didn't know what I was supposed to do. They walked off, the woman talking, but the man was still shaking his head. I watched as they drove away.

I tried to get Sam to play with me, but she didn't seem very interested. Most of the time she didn't even want to eat her dinner. Once in a while, the lady who picked us up in the truck would open a kennel door and take my friends out for people to see. They would be petted, and sometimes picked up and held. I wanted someone to pick me up. The people and my friends would walk out together and get in a car and drive away. I thought they were so lucky!

A couple of days later, the woman and the man who visited before came back, and they had the lady who drove the truck with them. Maybe they were coming to see Sam and me. They walked my way, and the next thing I knew, the truck lady was opening my cage door. My heart was pounding wildly. They patted me on the head, picked me up and I gave the woman a lick. She smelled so good. The man was talking, but he didn't seem to know what he wanted. They put me back in the cage and walked down the aisles looking at my other friends. Then they came back. The truck lady took me out of the cage and put a rope around my neck.

As we walked away I notice the truck lady didn't open Sam's cage. *Wait! What about my friend Sam! You can't leave her here.* I tried not to walk, but they were dragging me. I kept looking back at Sam. She was my friend, I couldn't leave her here. The nice woman stopped and talked to the man. He shook his head no and kept pulling me along. They took me down the ramp and into an office where they filled out paperwork and paid for me. As we were getting ready to get into the car, I kept pulling at my new leash, pulling towards the kennels where Sam was barking and running up and down the cage wildly.

The truck lady kept looking at her watch and seemed impatient, as it was almost closing time. The man and woman talked to each other some more. Then, all three of us went back inside where Sam was jumping up and down at the kennel door. I couldn't believe it! The man motioned for the truck lady to open Sam's cage door. As the door opened, Sam jumped into the man's arms and gave him a big kiss. The man nodded yes and smiled at the woman. They took Sam and me back into the office and repeated the same procedure.

Sam and I and the nice couple all got into the car and went to our new home. That night as we were cuddling up in our warm beds to go to sleep, we overheard the man and woman talking. They were talking about how the truck lady told them they were planning to take me and Sam on one of those walks out the back door. The same ones we saw our friends go on that never returned. Our walk was scheduled for the following morning❧

∾ A STARTLING STATISTIC ∾

Approximately one dog is euthanized every six seconds in the United States.

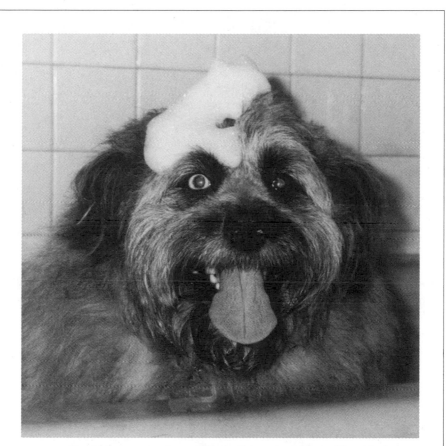

Taz is the companion of Linda Steger in Atlanta, Georgia.

Taz

❦ ❦ ❦

"The great pleasure of a dog is that you may make a fool of yourself
with him and not only will he not scold you,
but he will make a fool of himself too."

SAMUEL BUTLER

Photo © Richard Thomas

Shannon Marshall and Cassie

Cassie
A GIRL'S BEST FRIEND
–Shannon Marshall, Georgia

My dog, Cassie, and I have a very special relationship. Every morning, she'll come up to the side of my bed and start to nudge my hand to wake me up—she's like my second alarm clock. Every school day, Cassie goes along for the ride to school in the van with me and my mom. Mom's driving, I'm sitting next to her, and Cassie is right between us.

Our backyard has a steep hill in it, and when I was younger, it was hard for me to climb back up the hill once I went down. Cassie was always there to help out, offering her tail for me to hold onto as she pulled me back up the hill.

Cassie has been my constant companion for all of my twelve years. She has always taken good care of me, and now that she is almost blind and deaf, I take extra care of her. She is absolutely the best mutt ever! ❧

Susan Miller

Olivia

ALL EARS

—In Livvy's words, as told to: Susan Miller, Connecticut

Hi, my name is Olivia. My friends call me Livvy for short, but I've also been called "rat dog," and "Yoda" because of my giant ears. Well, they can call me whatever they like. I know I'm beautiful because I'm the best dog of all—a mutt! 🐾

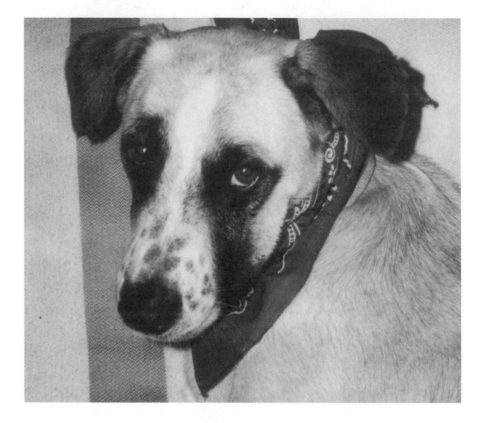

Buddy

From Rags to Riches

—In Buddy's words, as told to: Todd Manion, Florida

It was a Saturday morning. I woke up under my favorite old Ford pickup truck. It wasn't a bad place to live. There was plenty of soft grass underneath, and it was backed up to a fence that had overgrown bushes so it stayed nice and cool. I crawled out from under the truck and stretched. It was pretty quiet around the warehouse. See, I'm kind of the resident dog at a storage warehouse, you know, garage after garage, row after row. It gets used by a variety of people, from families storing furniture, to rock and roll bands. Well, that's where my friend Todd comes in.

You see, I was carrying my favorite dog food can around when I met him. He was always so nice to me, and would give me lots of attention. He even used to let me in his band's room sometimes to listen to them play. I really like all the guys in his band. Even though I was pretty greasy and grimy, they still let me in. Fleas were a bit of a problem too, but they didn't seem to mind.

I had an old rope tied around my neck for a collar, so Todd went out and bought me a fancy leather collar. Once I remember him giving me a bath with a hose out back, he must have thought I needed it. I couldn't remember the last time I had one.

I guess I had been in the parking lot of that place for about eight months when Todd decided enough was enough. On that particular night my life changed forever. It was raining cats and dogs. Todd had let me into the room because I was soaked to the bone. He was getting ready to leave, and as he was pulling away, I was crammed against the door to the garage so I could stay out of the rain. Todd looked at me and me at him, then all of the sudden I noticed the side door to his van open. He called out, "Come on, Buddy." I couldn't believe it. I jumped in that van so fast it made my tail spin!

The next thing I knew, I was getting bathed, fed, and loved beyond my wildest dreams. No more parking lots for me, no sir. It's all couches and beds from now on.❖

❖ ❖ ❖

"Nobody can fully understand the meaning of love unless they've had a dog. A dog can show you more honest affection with a flick of his tail than a person can gather through a lifetime of handshakes."

GENE HILL, "THE DOG MAN"

Christine Curry Young

Benji is the companion of Christine and Raymond Young of New York.

Benji

"Never judge a dog's pedigree by the books he does not chew."

ANONYMOUS

© Rouse Elliott Photographers, DeKalb, Illinois

Dude

HEALER FOR A TROUBLED HEART

–Sharon Pflaumer, Illinois

More than a decade ago, my husband adopted a rangy Australian cat-
tle dog mix from a stable owner who planned to eliminate the dog by
planting a shotgun shell between his furry ears. It seems that "Dude"
was an incorrigible fighter with other dogs, couldn't be called off when
herding the horses, and chewed his way out of any enclosure.

Having already given a home to several hard-luck cases of non-pedi-
greed ancestry in the past, I hadn't really wanted another mutt. This
time, I had hoped to get a golden retriever that I could show. However,
I relented to my husband's wishes and the wild canine Houdini took
up residence with us.

Because Dude had been raised in the freedom of a barn, he didn't have a clue as to what it meant to be a house dog. The first time I left him home alone all day while I was at work, I came home to find a "Dude" sized hole in the door as well as complete and utter devastation inside the house. The weatherproofing plastic on every window was punctured and torn, the sorry contents of a garbage bag had been dragged across the floor, two curtain panels were partially severed, and my rattan magazine basket looked like lunch-time leftovers from some reptilian zoo specimen. And that was only the front porch!

Despite Dude's behavior problems, it was difficult not to be touched by his unsolicited devotion. Although my husband had adopted him, Dude inexplicably attached himself to me, and was always at my heels fawning for attention. He was there when I vacuumed and dusted and took out the trash. When I fed the horses and cleaned their stalls he pranced around behind me. And, if I picked wild asparagus behind the house, or gathered fruit in the orchard, he peeked up at me through his bandit-like face mask as he lay on the grass.

Although in our early days together Dude seemed intent upon destroying the house and most of my possessions, he did manage to repair something else that no one else could fix at the time—my troubled heart. You see, Dude arrived on the scene shortly before my marriage ended in divorce, and his endless outpouring of love was like a soothing balm on the raw nerve endings that my emotions had become.

As a result, I grew very fond of the trouble-seeking but nonetheless endearing Dude. In spite of the tumultuous things happening in my life, each day after work I raced home to feed and groom him. Then, I took him for a long walk in the pasture and the adjacent unplowed fields, or for a ride in the car to get a soft-serve ice cream cone.

In this way, Dude led me a little farther away from the pain of my broken marriage with each passing day, until almost without me realizing it, the dark times were well behind us. For this, I will always be grateful, and Dude, who will soon celebrate his fourteenth birthday, will always be my beloved and treasured friend.❖

Sammy
A CHARMING TERROR
—The Swartz Family, Florida

Sammy is a twenty-eight pound ball of cotton fluff in perpetual motion. If we do not pay enough attention to him, he will grab something he knows is dear to us and streak through the house. It always takes two people or one person and a "treat" to retrieve items such as underwear, our son's favorite stuffed animal, or important papers. One night Grandma and Grandpa stayed over, and the next morning Grandma let out a shriek as Sammy jumped up on the nightstand and made off with her teeth. The last thing he needs is another set of choppers!

Although Sammy is a bit of a terror at times, he more than makes up for it with his loving disposition and charm. After owning a pure-bred and spending a small fortune on vet bills, we are proud to own a mutt who only requires annual vaccinations. We couldn't have created a better dog if we tried🐾

Beanie, Tripod, and Elvis are the companions of Chris Dane of California.

Beanie, Tripod, Elvis

❧ ❧ ❧

"Mutt owners already know something that fancy breeders do not:
Papers and pedigrees are about dollars and cents. A mutt is about love."

JULIE MARS, AUTHOR OF *Mutts*

Frankie

Outwitting the Fates

—Robin Downing, DVM, Colorado

In March 1995, I had a call from two of my clients who volunteer for the Max Fund, a pet rescue group in Denver. They had rescued a little pug mix that had been run over by a car. He couldn't walk and needed a place to have physical therapy. With time and a little help, they thought he would walk again.

When the dog arrived at my veterinary hospital, we saw that his trauma was much more severe than his rescuers realized. It turned out that he had never had X-rays taken of his damaged spine. In a way, that oversight probably spared his life. Had any veterinarian seen his crushed and deformed spine at the time of his injury, he probably would have been euthanized. By the time we met him, however, this nine-pound wonder had lived with his injury for almost two months. His spinal cord had been crushed in the accident, rendering him a paraplegic.

I broke the news to his rescuers as gently as I could that the little guy would never walk again. Then the discussion began of what would happen to him next. It seemed so unfair to issue a death sentence to a dog that had already outwitted the fates—first the vehicle that struck him and then weeks of pain and healing without a complete diagnosis. So euthanasia was out of the question. After further discussion we decided it made sense for the dog to live at our clinic where we could attend to his bodily functions. We would do all we could to ensure him a comfortable and normal dog's life. None of us realized at that moment what a far-reaching effect our decision would have.

It was the fiftieth anniversary of FDR's death. To honor this little dog's tenacity and remind ourselves of the depth of human adaptability, we named him Franklin Delano Roosevelt. After all, that guy was paralyzed and he was president of the United States. Who knew where a little paralyzed dog could go? We called him Frankie for short.

Within a few weeks of Frankie's arrival, we had a custom-made wheelchair delivered to the clinic for him. The wheelchair changed Frankie's life. It gave him the same mobility as other dogs. Within six months he wore all the tread off his tires and needed new ones. The people at the K9 Cart Company, who make the wheelchairs, were puzzled about my request for new tires after such a short time. But they didn't know Frankie. He can walk for miles in his wheelchair, despite having front legs that are only four inches long. It took him eight months to wear out his next set of tires.

I have to help Frankie go the bathroom each day, but we have a regular routine. I am able to apply pressure with my hands against his bladder to help him urinate, and I apply pressure to his colon to stimulate a bowel movement. Because we do his "elimination routine" at very regular intervals, I don't need to worry that he will leak at an inopportune moment.

Self-esteem is never a problem for Frankie. He is happy to share his story with anyone willing to pay attention to him. He has become something of a goodwill ambassador and "poster boy" for animals with disabilities and special needs. His paralysis is obvious, even when he's not in his wheelchair. At times he scoots along the floor with his rear legs behind him like a tadpole.

I travel around the country lecturing about animals with special needs and Frankie often accompanies me to many of my lectures. He helps me explain that dogs can have medical problems that require long-term care and still lead very active, comfortable, and high quality lives.

Not only is Frankie a wonderful spokesdog for animals with special needs, he is also a great spokesdog for mutts. He weighs in at a mere nine pounds, is longer than he is tall, and has a smashed in face that prompts people to ask if it was damaged in an accident. He's part pug and part, well, that part we don't know—perhaps Pekinese. There couldn't be a better example than Frankie of why people need to look beyond physical appearances or pedigrees when it comes to dogs❧

Ziggy

PRICELESS MUTT

—Mary Campbell, Georgia

I couldn't ask for a better companion than my little Ziggy. We have a very special bond, and she has brought me so much happiness and love. I wouldn't trade my mutt for anything! 🐾

Lauren Chabina

Pepper and Buster are the companions of Lauren Chabina of New York.

Pepper

∿ AMAZING ANIMAL FACT ∿

Believe it or not, cats and dogs are distant relatives. They are both descendants of the same tree-dwelling creature known as Meircis who lived fifty million years ago.

Patricia B. Pasquarett

Cosmo

ROYAL HAWAIIAN POI

—*Patricia Pasquarett, Pennsylvania*

My husband, Mike, is an active duty colonel in the U.S. Army. Stationed on Oahu, he worked long hours while I was carrying a heavy class load to complete my college degree. Since our schedules didn't coincide we each spent many hours at home alone. We both yearned for someone to talk to during those lonely hours, a friend who would understand our limitations, yet wanted to share our lives. We always had our cat, Guido, but we needed more interaction than he could offer.

We decided perhaps a dog could benefit most from this untried yet hopeful situation. The minute we saw Cosmo at the humane society, it was love at first sight. However, that didn't last for long. We were totally unprepared for puppyhood. Little Cosmo insisted on expressing himself with pen in mouth on more than one oriental rug, shredding unguarded undies with glee, and perhaps his most grievous crime, tormenting poor Guido. To that end, after many tears and great angst, we returned Cosmo to the humane society due to incorrigible behavior.

However, Cosmo's cunning had already worked its magic. The very next day, totally unplanned, Mike showed up at the humane society at the same time that I was reclaiming this little bundle of sweetness and terror. We were afraid that Cosmo might not want to go with us since we'd returned him once already, but he was completely forgiving and let us back into his heart with no grudges held.

Cosmo is twice adopted, but also doubly loved. He keeps us balanced and more aware of what real life is about. He finds treasure in the simplest things and is blessed with an internal clock that rivals Greenwich mean time. He is an expert ball player, scoring high in soccer, football, baseball, and especially tennis. Frisbee, however is his absolute favorite.

People are always asking what type of dog Cosmo is. His lineage is a mystery that probably the keenest dog genealogists couldn't figure out. We just tell people that he is our very own "Royal Hawaiian Poi" dog, (Poi is the Hawaiian term used for mutts.) The usual response we receive from admirers is "Oh, I know that breed, but have never seen one. Do you know where I can get one?" ❧

Lathos is the companion of Sally Nettleton of Connecticut.

Lathos

❧ ❧ ❧

*"Money will buy a pretty good dog, but it won't buy
the wag of his tail."*

JOSH BILLINGS

Rose Ann Cariello

Petey is the companion of Rose Ann Cariello of New York.

Petey

❧ ❧ ❧

"If a dog will not come to you after he has looked you in the face, you should go home and examine your conscience."

WOODROW WILSON

David Greene

Kula and David Greene

Kula

THE ULTI-MUTT

—David Greene, New York

The term "mutt" normally has a bad connotation, but not to me. I wouldn't trade my beautiful mutt for any purebred. I love her too much. I once saw a bumper sticker that read "The more I'm around people, the more I love my dog." I laughed when I saw it, but now I believe it.🐾

Sharon Davis

Nemo is the companion of Sharon Davis of Minnesota.

Nemo

❧ A STARTLING STATISTIC ❧

Only one out of four dogs in the United States ever finds a permanent home.

Kathy Hayden

Wileen and Don Akers with Barney

Barney

LUNCHBOX THIEF

—Wileen and Don Akers, Tennessee

Barney has always had a propensity for gathering food. Many a time he has slipped off to the local Kroger, and come home with a loaf of bread, a pizza (still in the cellophane), and a package of sweet rolls.

One day he came up our driveway carrying a lunch bag that included a sandwich, a pack of Fritos, and an apple. We think he must have lifted it from one of the construction workers at a nearby shopping center.

One of the biggest joys of all is coming home from work each day and finding Barney "smiling" through the glass door. He actually curls his lip over his teeth and smiles at us! 🐾

Bandit

Office Fashion Hound

—Craig Williams, Florida

I went to the humane society with specific instructions to find a small, short-haired female dog. Much to my wife's immediate chagrin, I returned with a medium-sized, long-haired male terrier and beagle mix. He was ridden with mange and ear mites, and had looked so woefully from the cage. He was next on the chopping block, a stray they had named Festus. We wound up calling him Bandit because he completely stole our hearts.

From a stray of unknown origin, Bandit has risen to CEO of a small law office, which he runs with a firm paw. He is known as the office fashion hound, wearing a different bow tie for each day of the week. After a long day at the office, Bandit needs a walk along the beach to unwind and socialize with his friends. After his grueling schedule, tummy rubbing is in order, and then it's off to bed, where he's gently tucked in and covered with his favorite "blanky."

While we've often wondered about Bandit's past, and what his life was like before we adopted him, we are certain of one thing—he is truly an angel sent to enrich our lives beyond measure❖

Julie Williams

Bandit and Craig Williams

Abigail is the companion of Sue Allsop of South Carolina.

Abigail

❧ A Second Chance ❧

My family brought me home, cradled in their arms.
They cuddled me and smiled at me and said I was full of charm.
They played with me and laughed with me and showered me with toys.
I sure do love my family, especially the girls and boys.
The children loved to feed me, they gave me special treats.
They even let me sleep with them all snuggled in the sheets.
I used to go for walks, often several times a day.
They even fought to hold the leash, I'm very proud to say.
These are the things I'll not forget—a cherished memory.
I now live in the shelter, without my family.
They used to laugh and praise me when I played with that old shoe.
But I didn't know the difference between the old ones and the new.
The kids and I would grab a rag, for hours we would tug.
So I thought I did the right thing when I chewed the bedroom rug.
They said I was out of control, and would have to live outside.
This I did not understand, although I tried and tried.
The walks stopped, one by one; they said they hadn't time.
I wish that I could change things, I wish I knew my crime.
My life became so lonely in the backyard on a chain.
I barked and barked all day long to keep from going insane.
So they brought me to the shelter but were embarrassed to say why.
They said I caused an allergy, and then each kissed me good-bye.
If only I'd had some classes as a little pup.
I wouldn't have been so hard to handle when I was all grown up.
"You only have one day left," I heard the worker say.
Does this mean I have a second chance? Do I go home today?

—ANONYMOUS

Susie

CHAPTER TEN

Mutt Memorials

Years ago it was unheard of to publicly mourn the loss of a pet. But things have changed. Today there are an estimated five hundred pet cemeteries in the United States, and dozens of pet loss support groups and counselors. About twelve years ago, the International Association of Pet Cemeteries declared the second Sunday of September as Pet Memorial Day. Memorial events and ceremonies are held in observance of this special day throughout the country.

The following pages include a collection of touching memorials to some truly one-of-a-kind dogs. Some stories were received from submissions, while others were discovered through my research.

◆ ◆ ◆

Susie
1945–1959
GRIEF COUNSELOR

The first pet cemetery, and the largest in the United States, is Hartsdale Pet Cemetery in New York—founded in 1896 by Dr. Samuel Johnson, a famous Manhattan veterinarian. To date, more than seventy thousand pets have been laid to rest at Hartsdale. Although the cemetery is not exclusively for dogs, it originally started out as Hartsdale Canine Cemetery, and the majority of pets buried there are dogs.

Among the thousands of mutts buried at Hartsdale, there is one headstone of particular importance. It reads: "The little lady of dignity who led the burial procession. She comforted others in their sorrow, we will all miss you, Hartsdale Pet Cemetery." So, it couldn't be more fitting to give Susie, the "Hartsdale First Lady," the honor of leading the procession into this chapter of Mutt Memorials. The spirit of Susie still watches over and comforts those who mourn the passing of their beloved and irreplaceable mutts.

After Dr. Johnson passed away in 1942, George and Irene Lassen acquired ownership of Hartsdale. Three years later, one of the plotholders called to tell them about a stray dog she had found, and asked if they might be interested in taking the dog. The Lassens were still grieving the loss of their dog, Terri, and hadn't planned on having another dog so soon. But it was love at first sight when they saw the little terrier and beagle mix, and they took the dog home that day.

At first they thought the dog was all black, but after a good bath they were surprised to see her emerge mostly white with brown ears and a brown face mask. Apparently she had gotten into a coal bin in the basement. They named her Susie, and since they weren't sure of her exact birthdate, they decided her birthday would coincide with that of their young son, Ray. Every October there was a double celebration in which Susie had her own decorated cake complete with candles.

From the beginning, Susie seemed to realize that she lived in a special place, and that the people whom she came into contact with had special needs. She showed unusual dimensions of understanding. She became the cemetery's official greeter, and usually greeted stranger and friend alike with a sense of comforting familiarity.

Susie began leading the burial processions as pets' caskets were carried to their final resting places. During the prayer ceremony, she would bow her head in prayer along with others, and sometimes lean her head back and let out a mournful howl. "She had this uncanny sense. I don't know how, but it was like she knew exactly what to do," recalled Irene Lassen. "People used to think we taught her to do these things, but we never did. She just took it upon herself."

1945 SUSIE 1959
THE LITTLE LADY OF DIGNITY
WHO LED THE BURIAL PROCESSION
SHE COMFORTED OTHERS
IN THEIR SORROW
WE ALL MISS YOU
HARTSDALE CANINE CEMETERY

Susie's headstone

Susie had free run of the grounds, but never once attempted to leave. It was her duty to be there, always on-call to comfort those who had just lost their beloved pets. She spent most of her days inside the office with George Lassen, but as soon as she heard someone coming, she'd run out to greet them. "Whenever anyone came to the office, it was usually a sad event," noted Irene. "Susie sensed this, and would often go outside and sit on the bench next to people as they grieved their loss. They appreciated her so much."

Plotholders who came to visit often brought treats and gifts for Susie. At holiday time she received dozens of Christmas cards, and throughout the year people sent her postcards and letters. "One time a package came air mail addressed to 'Ms. Susie.' We got a real kick out of that, and Susie sure enjoyed the package since it was filled with doggie biscuits," recalled Irene.

Susie's friends spread far and wide. She was written about in newspapers, and thousands of people took memories of her home with them to all parts of the country. Among Susie's admirers was one particularly ardent individual who lived across the street from the cemetery—a cocker spaniel named Taffy. Whenever Taffy's owners couldn't find him, they felt certain that he and Susie were wandering through the grounds of the cemetery paying their respects.

Susie touched the lives of all who came to the cemetery for the fourteen years she lived there. She helped shape the cemetery's history with her unique contributions, and is regarded as a beloved historical figure.

In 1959, Susie died after a short bout with cancer, and was buried in a private ceremony just for the immediate family. They were too grief-stricken at the time to notify anyone else of her death.

Susie was laid to rest beside a dogwood tree, where she was later joined by the Lassen's next dog, a German shepherd named Charmaine. After Charmaine was buried, the dogwood tree in between her and Susie bloomed twice that year, in spring and fall. But the blossoms were strangely distorted, unlike any blossoms that had ever bloomed on the tree before. The following year the tree died, and any tree that was plant-ed in its place after that never grew. To this day, Irene and her family believe that this strange chain of events was a result of Susie and Charmaine playing tricks on them ❧

Courtesy of Hartsdale Pet Cemetery

❧ ❧ ❧

"He came into my life for want of a meal and a place to stay...
he left with my heart."

INSCRIPTION ON A MONUMENT AT HARTSDALE PET CEMETERY

Lonesome Dog and Joe Ware

Lonesome Dog
1988–1995
A LOVE-FILLED LIFE
—Mary Pagel-Ware, Texas

In December 1988, a station wagon stopped at a country crossroad in Sealy, Texas, and booted a small brown dog onto the road. Thus began the story of one abandoned young dog and many caring people.

Lonesome Dog (named after the *Lonesome Dove* story) waited at that same corner week after week, hoping his owners would come back for him, but they never returned. One by one, local residents began leaving food and water for him, and made attempts to befriend the frightened dog. He would happily frolic with cows in adjoining pastures, but would not let humans get anywhere near him.

That winter turned bitter cold, and concern grew for Lonesome's safety. A caring couple down the road brought him a makeshift cardboard dog house covered in plastic, so he would be protected from the cold and rain. My friend at the time, Joe Ware (now my husband), took a special interest in Lonesome, and began visiting him every day. After

Mary Pagel-Ware

Lonesome's mailbox

a few weeks, Lonesome started following Joe down the road towards his house, going a little bit further each day. One day, after several months of daily visits, he followed Joe for five miles, all the way back to his house, and right into his backyard.

It took three days for Lonesome to trust Joe enough to allow him to remove a cloth belt tied to his neck when he was abandoned. But within a few weeks, Lonesome settled right in, and acted as if Joe's home had always been his home.

Realizing that many people would be concerned about Lonesome's whereabouts, Joe took an old mailbox from his house and planted it on the corner next to the cardboard dog house. He posted a note telling people where Lonesome could be found, and asked everyone to leave their names and numbers for a special celebration. Two letters actually went through the U.S. mail to Lonesome's box, and about twenty notes were left by caring friends.

A few weeks later, Joe and I threw a big party for all of Lonesome's friends. Everyone rejoiced that this once very lonely dog who would not go near a human, now had a loving, secure home. Lonesome lived seven love-filled years with Joe, until he died of kidney failure in January 1995 ❖

Courtesy of Colorado Department of Transportation

Shep
1950–1964
COLORADO'S TURNPIKE MASCOT

It's hard not to notice the small, obviously pampered, solitary burial site that stands on a hillside along the south side of U.S. 36 near Boulder, Colorado. Every so often, visitors can be seen stopping to pay their respects or to leave flowers. Some have attached American flags to the railing surrounding the grave site, while others have left biscuits, rawhide bones, and small dog toys.

For more than twelve years, a gentle collie mix named Shep lived outside the toll booth on the Boulder Turnpike. Some say that he was abandoned as a puppy by a local family who moved away, while other stories have it that that a toll road construction worker left him behind when he was transferred to another job.

Shep first appeared when the Boulder-Denver Turnpike was still under construction in 1950. He was a shy and fearful young puppy, and mostly lurked in the background, waiting for workers to toss him bits of their lunches. Each day he came a little closer, but not close enough for the workers to touch or pet him.

As time went on, Shep began to gain trust in the workers, and soon adopted them as his family. By the time the toll booth was completed in 1952, Shep was a familiar fixture at the site, and shortly after the groundbreaking ceremony, he took up residence outside the booth.

He spent his days basking in the sun on the curb of the booth, and keeping the toll operators company. Whenever a toll worker arrived to begin their shift, Shep would run out to greet them. All of the workers loved Shep, and always looked forward to seeing him each day. His friendship and companionship made those long hours sitting in the booth much more enjoyable.

At first Shep refused invitations to sleep inside the booth at night, and spent many bitter cold winter nights outside. But eventually he accepted the invitation, and from then on spent most nights curled up inside the warm booth. Shep became the official turnpike mascot, and in 1954 and 1955 his photo appeared on the state's annual report for the turnpike.

Vacationers to the area always remembered Shep, and brought him toys and treats when returning each year. Many people just passing through would pay 50¢ instead of the 25¢ toll with instructions to "keep the change for Shep." One time a man passed through and took out a whole case of dog food and gave it to the toll operator. He was a dog food salesman and told them he would be glad to refill the supply whenever Shep ran out. Each year at Christmas time, Shep received hundreds of cards from around the country, sometimes with money tucked inside to buy him special treats or toys.

On special occasions, local highway patrol officers would take Shep in their car to Boulder for a special treat or hamburger. He always recognized the black and whites, and as soon as an officer pulled up to the booth, he jumped in the car without a moment's hesitation.

When Shep occasionally got himself into trouble, veterinarian Clyde Brunner was always there to patch him up free of charge. One day, toll collectors were shocked to find Shep lying in the grass with a shotgun blast to his right front leg. Apparently a nearby farmer didn't take kindly to Shep chasing some of his animals. Dr. Brunner treated the wounded leg and set it in a cast.

Shep's shooting caused such upset among turnpike travelers that the story soon appeared in newspapers around the country. Get well cards and letters started pouring in from everywhere, several containing money to help with Shep's recovery. Word has it that eventually a checking account was opened at a local bank just for Shep.

As the years went by, age crept up on Shep. He became deaf and blind and his arthritis caused him so much pain that toll collectors often had to carry him around. His several bouts with coyotes over the years hadn't helped matters either. Paul Kempf served as the tollbooth superintendent for several years while Shep was the resident mascot. He was closest of all to Shep, and had to make one of the toughest decisions of his life in the summer of 1964 when he took his beloved friend to Dr. Brunner's to be euthanized.

By the time Paul returned, one of the maintenance workers had already dug a grave for Shep. They laid their friend to rest on a hill overlooking his beloved home, the toll booth. When word of Shep's death reached the newspapers, donations came in from around the country to pay for a proper memorial. Enough money was collected to erect two marble gravestones and a wrought-iron railing that surrounds the grave site. His gravestone reads: "Part Shepherd, Mostly Affection."

Shep's legend has lived on for more than thirty years and will continue to do so for years to come in the hearts of people in Broomfield, and around the country who knew him. He touched the lives of thousands who have never forgotten him❧

Zak
1970–1984
A ONE-OF-A-KIND DOG

For fourteen years photographer, Jane Lidz, shared her life and many wonderful adventures with her dog, Zak. She found Zak at an animal shelter in Colorado when he was just an eight-week old puppy. "I fell totally in love with his face," recalled Jane. The two moved several times throughout the years, finally settling in Northern California.

"As Zak grew, he seemed to change almost daily. I never knew what to expect next," admitted Jane. "He was a Heinz 57 with a lion's coat, a pig's tail, a terrier stubbornness and a heart of gold. He was the most loving, outgoing, charming, and intelligent dog you would ever meet." Jane kept a photographic record of Zak over the years. "He was so full of expressions—a dog with a thousand faces, and I took thousands of photos," she recalled.

After Zak died in 1984, Jane wanted to memorialize her longtime companion. She came up with the idea for a book about Zak after recalling how people would constantly stop her to ask "What type of dog is that?"

In 1996, *Zak: The One-Of-A-Kind Dog*, was published. In a most charming and delightful book written from the dog's point of view, Zak sets off on a journey to discover his origins. During his travels, he encounters a cast of characters, including children and other animals, who help him discover the joy of simply being himself.

About mid-way through his journey, Zak is pictured with a little girl he met along the way, looking up at a dog breed chart with the caption reading "I'm not even on the dog chart." At the end of his journey, Zak decides there is nothing he'd rather be than a "one-of-a-kind dog." The book ends with a closeup shot of Zak's expressive face, and the caption reading, "What kind of person are you?"

Working with a magnifying glass and a toothpick, Jane meticulously hand-colored thirty photos for the book over the course of a year. "In some of the photos I could see the reflection of myself photographing Zak in his eyes. It was a very emotional, but wonderful experience," recalled Jane.❖

❖ ❖ ❖

"The biggest drawback to having a mutt is that you can never have another dog like it. They are all one-of-a-kind."

ANONYMOUS

Sissy
1983–1997
THE POST-MUTT ALWAYS BARKS TWICE

For more than thirty-one years, Forest Catron has been delivering mail to the residents of Dorchester, Massachusetts—but he hasn't always done it alone. For fourteen of those years he was accompanied by his special friend and "co-worker," a dog named Sissy. Normally there might be cause for concern to see a dog following a mail carrier, but not in the case of Sissy and Forest. Theirs was a love affair between a friendly mutt and a kindly mailman.

The unlikely pair first met in the spring of 1983. Forest always made it a point to get to know the residents in the neighborhood, especially their dogs. He knew which ones were friendly and which ones were not. Each morning at 9:00 AM, he parked his mail truck outside the Feeney residence, where he began his route on foot. One morning, as he pulled up to park his truck, a small black puppy came running up to greet him. After inquiring with the Feeneys he found out the dog was theirs and they had just adopted her the day before. She was a sheepdog and collie mix, and her name was Sissy. Forest spent a few minutes petting the friendly pup, delivered the Feeney's mail, and went off on his way.

When Forest had gotten about a half a block away, Sissy came running up to him, wagging her tail excitedly. She followed alongside him for the next few blocks, then turned around and went home. The next day, when Forest drove up, Sissy was waiting out on the sidewalk to greet him. "She was so happy to see me. She really took to me from the start, and the feeling was mutual," recalled Forest. Over the next several months, Sissy followed Forest a little further each day, until eventually the two were walking the entire five-mile route together.

It was clear to see that Forest and Sissy had a special relationship. "She was friendly and liked other people, but she really worshiped Forest," explained Pat Foley, owner of a local florist shop. "She was very protective of him and he always watched out for her." Whenever they crossed busy streets, Forest always made sure Sissy was safely by his side; when it was hot outside, he made sure she had enough water to drink; and he always brought treats to give her at the end of his route. "She was really like my dog, even though she didn't live with me," recalled Forest. "I think Sissy was bored at home, and knew that I enjoyed her company."

The two became a familiar sight to many residents and businesses in the neighborhood who looked forward to seeing them each day. "Sissy would come in to say hi and get a drink of water, but she never paid any attention to the cat and bird we have in our shop, she was only concerned with Forest," noted Pat. The nearby pet shop always had treats or water for Sissy, while other business people and residents would come out just to greet her and Forest. In rain, sleet or snow, nothing would stop the pair from making their rounds.

When Forest went on vacation or had days off, Sissy had no interest in following substitute mail carriers. Sometimes though, she was seen walking the route by herself, looking for Forest. And when he returned, the two picked up right where they left off. "As soon as I'd pull up in my truck she was always right there, ready to go. And if I didn't get out fast enough for her, she'd just hop right inside the truck," stated Forest.

Although Forest had a job to do, he never let Sissy down. In her younger years it was no trouble for her to keep up the pace with Forest as he walked briskly, nearly jogging from house to house. But as she got older and began to slow down, Forest slowed down his pace so she could keep up with him.

In the fall of 1996, Sissy retired from her walks with Forest due to failing eyesight, hearing, and arthritis. It had been thirteen years since she first started walking the mail route with Forest. A year later she died at the age of fourteen. "I still miss her very much," lamented Forest. "She was a great companion to me, and although I've had other dogs in my life, none were as special as Sissy."

Fred
1978–1993
Nine Pounds of Devotion
–Nadine Bodnar, California

What can you say about nine pounds of fluff named Fred? Just that he was full of fun, energy, and love with the most special twinkling eyes you've ever seen. He was the cutest guy. Even people who didn't care for dogs (something I'll never understand), couldn't resist him. And believe me, he simply wouldn't have it any other way.

Fred was the love of my life and devoted companion for fifteen wonderful years. There was never a day in all that time that just looking at him, hearing him, thinking about him, or holding him didn't warm my heart and soul and make me smile. I lost him to cancer in 1993, and thinking of him still warms my soul, although now it's combined with a tear or two.

I will always be grateful for that phone call from my mother so many years ago telling me about a little dog wandering lost in a local shopping center. I drove to meet my mother at the shopping center, and the moment I laid eyes on him, my heart just melted. When I asked him if he would like to come home with me, I got a great big kiss across my face, and that was the beginning of a beautiful love affair.

Freddie remains the love of my life. He graced me with his presence and will always be greatly missed. There is nothing like a mutt, and certainly none like Freddie! ❧

Fred

Kathleen Laplante

Captain
1975–1983

A KEEPER OF THE HEART

–Kathleen LaPlante, New York

Captain was your basic black-and-white, formidable, but friendly, cat-loving, stay-at-home dog. It is easier to say that he simply was a great dog, rather than to try and tell anyone that he was the world to me, or that there never was, nor would there ever be, a dog quite like him.

Cappy was a farm dog; a keeper of the animals and a guardian of the grounds. He did this naturally, as though it were bred into him, sometime, somewhere; perhaps only as far back as being born on a working farm to a big, shaggy tri-colored collie-type father and a thin, nondescript, small black mother.

Cappy was one of us, an only dog for most of his years. He slept and ate with us, played with the kids, conversed with me daily, and took care of whatever animals we had. Thinking back, he was so much a part of us, I probably took it all for granted. I never gave it a second thought when Cappy got up each morning, went outside, circled the house, checked on the animals, and then did his business well outside of the immediate yard.

The last thing Cappy did before going to bed each night was to check on the chipmunk living in an aquarium in our bedroom. One day I had put a life-size stone chipmunk on the night stand between the bed and the aquarium. That night when we were turning in, Cappy went to check on the chipmunk in the aquarium. When he spotted the stone critter on the night stand, his eyes bulged out as if in disbelief. He shot a glance back to the aquarium, saw the chipmunk there, shot another glance over to the fake chipmunk, and walked over to sniff it. He'd been fooled! That incident and several others convinced me that dogs do think...if not all dogs, well, I believe Cappy did.

One of his favorite hobbies was fishing for minnows in the creek. He would spend hours at a time at the creek, right up to the winter, and when springtime came, he was back at it again. He had one other hobby, only I called it a bad habit. He had to chase the neighbor's truck. No means of discipline would stop him from chasing the truck—until I discovered the Mickey Mouse T-shirt method. When I put the T-shirt on him, he would hide or slink around, but would definitely not chase the neighbor's truck in a Mickey Mouse T-shirt! He was too proud.

The Captain had come into our lives on a wet and miserable, bone-chilling March day in 1975. When he left eight years later, it was on a warm, sunny summer's day. Perhaps he felt his work was done, as he padded off to the deserted flower garden and laid himself down beneath a long forgotten rosebush. It was there that I found him.

It has been fifteen years now, but I can gaze at my doorstep and picture him there, or when I hear thunder or a gun shot, I can see him scurrying to the house for safety. To this day, I can still see the Captain roaming the fields of home, and I know that I always will.❧

Fred
1979–1997
FOREVER YOUNG AT HEART
–Joanne Morgan

Our incredible life with Fred began when we rescued him in the summer of 1994. He was abandoned at a local business, which had closed unexpectedly. He had spent his entire life—fifteen and a half years at the time—at this location, and was even considered a part of the "inventory" when the business changed hands in 1991.

Despite his initial lack of training and socialization, Fred grew to become one of the best dogs we will ever get the chance to know. He was the oldest canine member of Animals at Risk Care Sanctuary, and was the Master of Ceremonies at our "Doggie Walk" in 1996.

In January 1997, we celebrated Fred's eighteenth birthday by holding a party for him at the Modesto Centre Plaza. We invited the public and all of his favorite people, canine, and feline friends. He made many new friends that night when people from the community stopped by to bring him gifts and good wishes. The menu included carrot cake for the guest of honor and his friends. People were amazed to find out that Fred was eighteen, considering his size and likely heritage. He was a very large dog—a mixture of Great Dane, Rhodesian ridgeback and shepherd, none of which normally lives much past ten to twelve years, and very rarely, if ever, to eighteen!

In July 1997, our beloved Fred was diagnosed with cancer. He passed away that October, and left a void in all of our hearts that will probably never be filled. Despite his age and terminal illness, he acted much younger than his eighteen years, until just before his death. He was such a special friend and one of those unique dogs who graced all of our lives with his "Fredness."

Before his death in the summer of 1995, we established the "Fred Fund," to assist other elderly and disabled pets who have been abandoned like Fred was. As a result, many homeless pets have become a part of our Continuing Care program, and will reside at the Retirement Home to live out their remaining years in comfort. After Fred's death, we changed the name to the "Fred Memorial Fund," and a book about his life story titled *Life With Fred* is currently being written❖

❖ ❖ ❖

"You think dogs will not be in heaven?
I tell you they will be there long before us."

ROBERT LOUIS STEVENSON

Chief

THE PROTECTOR

—Susan Burian, New York

Chief came to live with us after his previous owners neglected to care for him. He was the local "tough guy" neighborhood dog. He would run loose and all of the other dogs were afraid of him. He traveled around from house to house—mine included—looking for handouts or just to visit. This went on for a number of years. Eventually Chief began spending more and more time with us, and we became very attached to him.

One day, a small terrier who lived next door, came into our yard and attacked our poodle, Fudgie. Chief came out of nowhere and grabbed the terrier by the throat, flipped him on his back and held him there until we told him to "let go." No one was hurt, and Chief was declared a hero.

It came to a point where Chief's owners had neglected him so much that we decided it was time to intervene. We adopted him and his former owner didn't even care. In fact they were glad. Chief adjusted very well to becoming a house dog, and lived out his later years content and much loved. He was the type of dog who would give his life to protect our family. Some people were afraid of him—he looked tough, but Chief was really a sweetie. We all miss him very much.❧

Mary A.R. Keally

Blackie was the companion of the Keally family of Georgia.

Blackie
1977–1996

"Dogs' lives are too short. Their only fault, really."

CARLOTTA MONTEREY O'NEIL

Resources

The Resources section was written with mutts in mind, however the majority of information featured here can be used by every dog lover.

❀ ACTIVITIES

❀ ADOPTION

❀ MUTT CLUBS

❀ MUTTS ON THE INTERNET

❀ ANNUAL EVENTS CALENDAR

❀ PRODUCTS, GIFTS, & MISCELLANEOUS

❀ RECOMMENDED READING

Note: As of February 1999, all information in this section is current.
If you know of any changes or additions, please contact NewSage Press.

Conrad aka "The Wonder Mutt," performing a back vault with his owner, William Linne, Director of the National Capital Air Canines in Washington, D.C.

ACTIVITIES

Whether your dog is just a puppy, or a canine senior citizen, there is something here for every mutt. Participating in these activities will give your dog a good opportunity to socialize with other dogs, and it's a great way for you to meet fellow mutt lovers and dog enthusiasts.

Listed below are brief descriptions and contact information for numerous activities and sports that you and your mutt can investigate. All of these activities also welcome purebred dogs.

Dog Play
http://www.dog-play.com/
Whether it's competitive or casual dog-related activities you're looking for, you'll find it all at this web site. Features hundreds of links to dog activity web sites, and dozens of informative articles on various activities.

COMPETITIVE ACTIVITIES

AGILITY

Agility is a competitive sport where dogs race against the clock while running through an obstacle course consisting of hurdles, tunnels, and ramps. If you want to teach your dog agility just for fun and not for competition, there are instructional books available.

Agility Books and Videos

Enjoying Dog Agility: From Backyard to Competition by Julie Daniels
Agility Training: The Fun Sport For All Dogs by Jane Simmons-Moake

Agility Organizations

U.S. Dogs Agility Assoc. (USDAA)
P.O. Box 850955
Richardson, TX 75085
(972) 231-9700
http://www.usdaa.com/
Free information packet available, including contact numbers for affiliated chapters in your area.

Agility Association of Canada (AAC)
638 Wonderland Road South
London, Ontario, Canada N6K 1L8
(519) 473-3410

North American Dog Agility Council (NADAC)
HCR 2, Box 277
St. Maries, ID 83861
(208) 689-3803
http://www.teleport.com/~jhaglund/nadachom.htm
Listings of clubs by region.

United Kennel Club
100 East Kilgore Road
Kalamazoo, MI 49001-5593
(616) 343-9020

Agility Web Sites

The Dog Agility Page
http://www.dogpatch.org/agility.html
Everything you want to know about agility. Numerous links to regional clubs, agility action photos, and events.

Dog Agility Page
http://cust.iamerica.net/dstar1/dogagility.htm
A very informative dog agility site with several links and photos.

FLYBALL

Flyball is a competitive relay race between two teams of four dogs each. Each dog jumps over the hurdles and steps on a spring-loaded box that shoots out a tennis ball. The dog catches the ball and then runs back over the four hurdles to the starting line where the next dog is waiting to go. The first team to have all four dogs run the course without errors wins.

Flyball Organizations

North American Flyball Association
(NAFA)
1400 W. Devon Avenue, Box 512
Chicago, IL 60660
Write for a copy of official flyball rules, or to locate teams in your area.

Mixed Breed Dog Club of America
13884 State Route 104
Lucasville, OH 45648-8586
(614) 259-3941

Flyball Web Sites

National American Flyball Association
http://muskie.fishnet.com/~flyball/flyball.html

NAFA's web site includes a variety of information on flyball. Features a search engine and "Locator Bulletin Board" to help you find a team in your area. Has links for numerous flyball team web sites.

Flyball Publications

Flyball Training...Start to Finish by Jacqueline Parkin
Flying High by Joan Payne
On Your Mark by Mike Randall

CANINE FRISBEE

Of all the canine competitive sports, Frisbee is the most amazing to watch. The dogs and handlers who compete in these matches are incredible acrobats. Whether you want to throw a few Frisbees with your dog in the backyard, or join an official "Dog Disc" team, the following resources will provide the information you need to get started.

Canine Frisbee Organizations

Alpo Canine Frisbee Disc Championships
4060-D Peachtree Rd., Suite 326
Atlanta, GA 30319
(800) 786-9240
Alpo sponsors regional competitions across the United States each year. Write or call for a schedule of events, and to get a free 20-page canine Frisbee training manual.

Canine Frisbee Web Sites

Mary Jo's Frisbee Dog Page
http://www.dogpatch.org/frisbee.html
Comprehensive site featuring links to individual Frisbee dog team web sites, action photos, and resources.

Canine Frisbee Books & Videos

Frisbee Dogs: How to Raise, Train and Compete by Peter Bloeme
Frisbee Dogs Video by Peter Bloeme
Frisbee Dogs: Throwing Video by Peter Bloeme
Alpo Canine Frisbee Disc World Finals by Peter Bloeme

MUSICAL FREESTYLE

Can your mutt do the mambo? If so, you might want to check this out. Musical freestyle is a relatively new sport that combines dog obedience and dance, presenting a visually exciting display of handler and canine teamwork. The handler and dog perform dance-oriented footwork in time to music.

Musical Freestyle Organizations

The Canine Freestyle Federation (CFF) is an international organization dedicated to defining and developing the sport of Canine Freestyle. Its web site lists phone numbers and addresses for contact people for classes or demonstrations in your area.
http://home.sprynet.com/sprynet/ k9trainer/homepage.htm

Pup-Peroni Canine Freestyle
Patie Ventre
4547 Bedford Avenue
Brooklyn, NY 11235
Phone: (718) 332-8336
Fax: (718) 646-2686
e-mail: PupFreesty@aol.com
Pup-Peroni sponsors musical freestyle demonstrations and competitions around the country. The Pup-Peroni Canine Freestylers travel nationwide giving demonstrations and seminars.

PUPPYDOG ALL STARS K9 GAMES

Puppyworks
(707) 745-4237 or (888) K9 GAMES
http://www.puppyworks.com.
e-mail:events@puppyworks.com
All Star K9 Games is the latest addition to the growing world of canine sports, founded by dog behaviorist and trainer, Ian Dunbar. K9 games include a mix of all of the dog sports listed here, and then some. "Musical Chairs" the "Doggy Dash," and the "Woof Relay," are some of the activities included.

CASUAL ACTIVITIES

DOG CAMPS

Yes, it's just like it sounds—camps for dogs. Dog camps are very similar in environment and activities to a typical children's summer camp, but the main difference here is that you can accompany your four-legged child to camp. This is a great way to meet other dog lovers, and a good chance for you and your dog to spend some quality time together. Contact the following camps for schedules and fees.

Camp Dances with Dogs
316 Creek Road
Frenchtown, NJ 08825
(908) 996-7346
e-mail: clothier@eclipse.net

Camp Gone to the Dogs
RR 1, Box 958
Putney, VT 05346
(802) 387-5673

Camp Winnaribbun
P.O. Box 50300
Reno, NV 89513
(702) 747-1561

Dog Days of Wisconsin
1879 Haymarket, No. 24
Waukesha, WI 53186
(414) 274-1749

Dog Scouts of America
5307 W. Grand Blanc Road
Swartz Creek, MI 48473
(810) 655-4129

DOG PARKS

In the past decade dog parks have been cropping up across the country at an amazing rate. Going to a dog park is a great way to get exercise for both you and your dog and to meet and socialize with fellow dog lovers.

Dog Park Web Sites

Dog Freeplay
http://www.freeplay.org/
PO Box 754 Venice CA 90294
Phone/Fax: 310-314-9600
e-mail: freeplay@gte.
An informative site for anyone interested in starting a dog park. Also has a listing of several dog parks across the country that have web sites.

Dog Runs & Parks
http://www.inch.com/~dogs/runs.html
Provides step-by-step information on how to set up a dog run or dog park.

Dog Run / Dog Park Reporter
http://www.mindspring.com/~patmar/in dex.htm
Includes information on locations for dog parks in California, Florida, and New York. Features comprehensive graphs for each park, listing the amenities the park or run includes like: shade, water, dog poop bags, etc.

THERAPY DOGS

As a dog owner, you know first hand about the unconditional love that dogs can give. By participating in Animal Assisted Therapy (AAT), you can share your dog's love with others who will greatly benefit from the companionship of an animal.

There are numerous AAT groups around the country to join. These groups organize regular visits to nursing homes, hospitals, children's facilities, etc. If you are interested in finding out more about AAT, or want to locate a group in your area, contact the following organizations.

Dog Therapy Organizations

Delta Society
Pet Partners Program
P.O. Box 1080
Renton, WA 98057-9906
(800) 869-6898, Fax: (425) 235-1076
http://petsforum.com/deltasociety/

Latham Foundation
Latham Plaza Blvd.
Clement & Schiller Streets
Alameda, CA 94501
(510) 521-0920, Fax: (510) 521-9861
e-mail: LATHM@aol.com
Contact for a complimentary publication on how to start a pet therapy program.

Paws For Friendship
P.O. Box 12243
Omaha, NE 68152
(402) 573-5826
http://www.probe.net/-paws4fsp
e-mail: paws4sfp@probe.net

Therapet
P.O. Box 1696
Whitehouse, Tx 75791-1696
(903) 842-4680
http://www.therapet.com/default.htm
e-mail: Therapet@juno.com

Therapy Dogs International
6 Hilltop Road
Mendham, NJ 07945
(201) 543-0888

Dog Therapy Web Sites

Therapy Dog Associations
http://www.rahul.net/hredlus/therapy.html
An extensive and comprehensive list of organizations and contacts for information on pet therapy.

Joining a Therapy Dog Group
http://www.dog-play.com/join.html
Another extensive, excellent list of groups and organizations for pet therapy. Includes brief descriptions on each organization and lists organizations by state.

Dog Therapy Books

Four Footed Therapist
by Janet Ruckert
Volunteering With Your Pet
by Mary Burch
Therapy Dogs
by Kathy Diamond Davis
Love on a Leash: Giving Joy to Others through Pet Therapy by Liz Palika

VOLUNTEERING

There are countless ways in which you can help provide the love and care that thousands of dogs desperately need each year, and to speak out on their behalf. Whether it's hands-on or behind the scenes work you are interested in, there are plenty of things you can do.

There are far too many organizations that have volunteer opportunities to list here, so I have provided a small list describing general volunteer opportunities available.

• **Donations:** Attend fundraising events sponsored by your local shelter or humane society, or hold your own fundraiser or garage sale. Shelters are always in need of supplies such as dog beds, toys, etc.

• **Fostering:** If you have available space and time, there are always dogs in need of temporary foster homes while waiting for a permanent one.

• **Humane Education:** There is a tremendous need for educating the public on important animal welfare issues such as spaying and neutering and animal abuse prevention. Numerous organizations offer humane education programs and are always in need of volunteers.

• **Shelter Volunteers:** Dog walking and socializing, clean-up, mobile pet adoptions, fundraising, and office help are just a few of the opportunities available at animal shelters and humane societies.

ADOPTION

Whether you are searching for a mixed-breed or purebred dog, please don't purchase one from a retail pet store. Stores that sell dogs continue to perpetuate the puppy mill and backyard breeder problem, where dogs are bred repeatedly in horrendous conditions.

There are thousands of wonderful, loving, and deserving dogs waiting for homes at animal shelters and humane societies across the country. Several resources are listed in this section to assist you in your search for a canine companion.

ADOPTION WEB SITES

With close to 6,000 animal shelters and humane organizations in the United States, it is impossible to list them all. The following web sites include individual organizations as well as linking sites to help you find a shelter or organization in your area.

Adoption Linking Sites

Canine Connections Breed Rescue
http://www.cheta.net/connect/canine/Rescue/
This page links to hundreds of breed rescue pages on the web listed in alphabetical order by breed. There is also a "Rescue Dog Listing" page that lists dogs who are currently in need of homes across the country. Each listing includes a brief description about the dog and links to the person's e-mail who is housing the dog.

Dog Infomat
http://www.doginfomat.com/dog04.htm
An excellent linking site. Features an extensive section containing links to shelters and rescue organizations, neatly organized by region and state.

Kyler Laird's Animal Rescue
http://www.ecn.purdue.edu/~laird/animal_rescue/shelters
Features a collection of animal rescue organizations and facilities that have a web presence. This site is continuously changing and is actively maintained. Also features shelters in England, Nova Scotia, and other places around the world.

Mercy Rescue Net
http://www.aaarf.org
A searchable database finds shelters and organizations located within a specified mile radius of your home. Only covers the Southern California area.

General Adoption Sites

Adoptable Dogs Web Site
http://www.access.digex.net/~rescue/DOGS/rocky.html
An excellent adoption site—very comprehensive and easy to navigate. Features several organizations in the Maryland suburbs of D.C. and the Baltimore-Washington corridor. Includes a chart that lists name of dog, breed mix, coloring, sex, age, and brief personality notes on dogs available for adoption.

Mixed-Breed Dog Rescue

http://www.interchem.com/rescue/
mixbreed.html
Dedicated to finding good homes for
rescued mixed-breed dogs nationwide.
They welcome advertisements for private party dogs needing homes and for
any mixed-breed rescue groups.

PAWS Progressive Animal
Welfare Society

http://www.paws.org/index.html
Features an abundance of articles, tips,
resources, and links. The pet adoption
page is updated daily and features photos and descriptions of pets. You can
even fill out an adoption form on-line
before visiting the shelter.

Pet Finder

http://www.petfinder.org/
Internet Directory of Homeless Pets in
the New Jersey area. Has pets for adoption from several organizations as well as
postings from private parties needing to
find homes for their pets. This site has its
own search engine that allows you to
search for adoptable dogs by sex, size,
age, and dominant breed (meaning, the
breed that it is a derivative of i.e. German
shepherd mix, etc.)

Save A Sato

http://www.northshore1.com/sato/
"Sato" is a slang term for "mixed breed
street animals" in Puerto Rico. The pri-
mary mission of Save a Sato is to
improve the quality of life for homeless
and abused companion animals on the
island of Puerto Rico. Some of the dogs
from this organization are available for
private adoption.

Senior Dogs Project

http://www.srdogs.com//
The Senior Dogs Project encourages and
facilitates the adoption of older dogs.
This site contains articles and information
on adopting an older dog, and also
includes articles on how to care for a senior dog.

MOBILE PET ADOPTION

If you can't make it to your local animal shelter to adopt a dog, then they
can come to you. Many shelters and
rescue groups now "set-up shop" at
local shopping malls, parks, or pet
supply retailers such as Petsmart and
Petco. To find out about mobile adoption events in your area, contact a
local adoption organization or call a
Petco, Petsmart, or local retailer.

PUREBRED DOG RESCUE

The pet overpopulation problem
has had a tremendous impact on
purebred dogs as well as mutts. An
estimated 25 percent (about two million) of all dogs entering U.S. animal shelters each year are purebred,
and thousands more are are waiting
in other facilities for a new home.

There are hundreds of "breed
rescue" organizations and individuals
devoted to rescuing dogs of a particular breed who have been turned into
animal shelters or otherwise relin-
quished by their owners.

Following are a few resources
that can help get you started on your
search for a purebred rescue dog.

On the Web

To find information on a particular
breed, go to one of the search engines
such as *http://www.yahoo.com* and type
in the breed you are interested in.

Project Breed
P.O. Box 15888
Chevy Chase, MD 20825-5888
(202) 244-0065
This organization publishes a directory of local, regional, and national rescue groups as well as details about what each group offers. The directory is updated on an annual basis and can be ordered by phone or mail.

Adoption Books

Adopting a Great Dog
by Nona Kilgore Bauer
Choosing A Shelter Dog
by Bob Christiansen
Save That Dog by Liz Palika
Saved! A Guide to Success With Your Shelter Dog by M.L. Papurt, DVM
Second Hand Dog
by Carol Lea Benjamiin
The Adoption Option
by Eliza Rubenstein & Shari Kalina
The Right Dog For You
by Daniel Tortora
Mutts: America's Dogs
by Brian Kilcommons, Mike Capuzzo

NATIONAL ORGANIZATIONS

Listed here are a few of the larger humane organizations that provide a variety of educational information and resources on pet adoption, pet care, spaying and neutering, dog rescue, and more.

American Human Association
63 Inverness Drive East
Englewood, CO 80112
(800) 227-4645
http://www. americanhumane.org
As a federation of more than 6,500 animal sheltering and protection agencies, AHA provides numerous grants, scholarships, and workshops to support the training of shelter staff and improvement of animal care facilities across the country.

ASPCA
American Society for Prevention of Cruelty to Animals
424 East 92nd Street
New York, NY 10128-6804
(212) 876-7700
http://www.aspca.org

Best Friends Sanctuary
5001 Angel Canyon Drive
Kanab, UT 84741-5001 USA
(801) 644-2001 Fax: (801) 644-2078
http://www.bestfriends.org
Best Friends is one of the largest no-kill animal sanctuaries in the country, housing more than 1,500 dogs, cats, rabbits, and other animals.

Doing Things for Animals
P.O. Box 2165
Sun City, AZ 85372-2165
(602) 977-5793
Publishes an annual directory that includes more than 300 listings for "No-Kill" animal shelters and sanctuaries around the country. To order, send $23 to address above.

HSUS
The Humane Society of the United States
2100 L Street, NW
Washington, DC 20037
(202) 452-1100
http://www.hsus.org

MUTT CLUBS

Currently there are only a handful of clubs that are exclusively for mutt enthusiasts. Hopefully the publication of this book and other pro-mutt books will encourage more clubs for mutts. Listed here are the clubs we have information on as of January 1999. If you know of any other clubs exclusively for mutts, please write to NewSage Press.

AMBOR
American Mixed Breed
Obedience Registration
10236 Topanga Blvd., 205
Chatsworth, CA 91311
(818) 887-3300
http://www.amborusa.org/
AMBOR was established in 1983 with the purpose of acknowledging the efforts and achievements of mixed-breed dogs. Tracking and obedience titles are earned at "fun matches" and events sponsored by training clubs or other breed clubs that allow mixed breeds to participate.

Mixed Breed Dog Clubs of America
Chris Dane
1118 Marquita
Burlingame, CA 94010
or Linda Lewis
13884 State Route104
Lucasville, OH
(614) 259-3941
The MBDCA was founded in 1978 in Washington State. There are currently three main chapters in California, Missouri, and Wyoming with individual members throughout the country. The organization promotes responsible dog ownership through obedience training, and strongly supports pet population control. Dogs eligible for membership include mixed-breeds, and breeds of any type that are physically handicapped, blind, or deaf.

North American Mixed Breed Registry
R.R.1
Baltimore, Ontario
K0K 1C0 Canada
Phone and Fax: (905) 342-3391
http://www.eagle.ca/~nambr/index.html
e-mail: nambr@eagle.ca
NAMBR was formed to meet the needs of and to unite mixed breed dog owners throughout North America. Membership to the group includes a bi-monthly newsletter.

"Sam"— Nancy Broerman, Grapevine, Texas

MUTTS ON THE INTERNET

Only a few web sites on the internet are mutt-specific, but there are thousands of sites that offer a wealth of information for every dog lover. Everything from adopting a dog to weekly astrological forecasts for your dog can be found on-line. Featured on the following pages are a variety of recommended sites to visit. If you know of any additional mutt-specific or other worthy dog-related sites, write to NewSage Press, or e-mail at: newsage@teleport.com.

MUTT SPECIFIC SITES

Cool Mutts Club
h*ttp://www.geocities.com/~misha_pups /coolmutt.html*
This is what is called a "Web Ring." It's not an actual web site, but an index to more than 400 web sites of individual dogs. The Cool Mutts web ring includes sites for both mutts and purebred dogs. But the club's president is a mutt named Misha, whose web page is included later in this section.

The disclaimer posted on this web ring is quite interesting, it reads: "The term 'Mutts' is used 'loosely' and is not meant in anyway to degrade any breed of dog or dogs. All dogs from mixed-breeds to championship purebred show dogs are all welcome to join the Cool Mutts Club Webring."

Cross Question
http://www.lightwave.co.uk/ dogs-today/comp.html
This is a page from the on-line version of a wonderful British magazine called *Dogs Today*. In each issue they feature a "Cross Question" competition, where readers guess what two breeds the featured mongrel (British term for mutt) is a mixture of.

Joy of Mutts
http://www.geocities.com/ Heartland/Hills/5441/

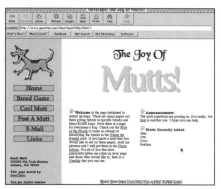

This site is truly a mutt lover's paradise! The Joy of Mutts is the largest and most extensive web site on the Internet dedicated entirely to mutts.

One of several fun activities on this site is the "Guess the Breed" game. Each month a different dog's photo is posted, and everyone tries their best guess as to what breeds the dog might be a mixture of. Other features on the site include: "Mutt of the Month," a photo album set up in alphabetical order, featuring more than 200 mutts' photos; a book store featuring selections of the latest books about mutts and dogs; and a message board where mutt enthusiasts worldwide can network and exchange stories.

Site creator, Ellen Chang, really knows her mutts, and has done an incredible job with the graphics and organization of this site. Ellen launched the site in April 1997, after being inspired by her own beloved mutt, Suzy, a lab, beagle, and dachshund mix.

Mutts Be Proud

http://members.wbs.net/homepages/m/ u/t/muttpride/ PRIDE.HTM
This site was just posted in November 1997. Although the grammar leaves a bit to be desired, the purpose of the site is a good one of course—to promote mutts.

Virtual Dog Show

http://www.dogshow.com/ fall98/catalog/
This is not a mutt-specific site, but they have a competition section devoted to mixed-breed dogs. This is an on-line version of a dog show, where people submit photos of their dogs to enter in various categories. Traditional categories such as "Best in Breed" and "Best in Show" are geared towards purebred dogs, but any dog can enter in categories such as: "Best in Activity," "Costume Party," "Dog/Owner Look-Alike," and "Rescue Dog."

GENERAL DOG SITES

All For Animals

http://allforanimals.com/
This site is mainly geared towards pet-related information for Santa Barbara, California. However, they have extensive information on national animal welfare organizations and events.

American Dog Trainer's Network

http://www.inch.com/~dogs/
This is one of the most resourceful and comprehensive dog web sites on the Internet. Nationally known dog trainer, Robin Kovary, has left no bone unturned in putting this site together. Although there are hundreds of links and informative articles related to dog training, this site includes much more than just dog training information. If you can't find the dog-related information you are looking for here, than it probably doesn't exist!

American Veterinary Medical Association

http://www.avma.org/default.htm
A variety of pet-health and pet care related information, as well as how to select a veterinarian, and a keyword search engine. You can also submit a story and photo about your dog that may be chosen and featured on the web site.

Cyber Dog

http://www.cyberpet.com/cyberdog/
Great graphics and very comprehensive. Plays the theme song from "Mission Impossible" when you enter the dog area. Great resource/linking site.

Dog Infomat

http://www.doginfomat.com/
An excellent linking page for dog-related sites. Includes an extensive section containing links to shelters and rescue organizations neatly organized by region and state.

Net Vet Dog Page

http://netvet.wustl.edu/dogs.htm
This page probably has the most dog links of any web site. However, they are alphabetically listed with no description, so you have to do a bit of hunting.

The Dogpatch Doghouse

http://www.dogpatch.org/dogs/
Features a variety of information on dog training, dog humor, dog products, and other various tidbits for dog lovers. Also features a large collection of useful dog links.

The Dog Hause

http://www.doghause.com/
An excellent all-around dog site. Neatly organized with great graphics.

WWW.Woof

http://www.woofs.org/frontp.html
An on-line dog publication. Has many interesting articles and stories, and lots of good links. Great photos and graphics.

JUST FOR FUN WEB SITES

Dog Biscuit and Treat Recipes

http://pages.prodigy.com/pomathon/pomtreat.htm
This is a page on the "Pomerama" web site for pomeranians, but any dog or mutt will love the tasty recipes here. Neatly categorized by beef, chicken, cheese, etc.

Pick a Hooman

http://vorlon.mit.edu/~melissa/cly/pick_hooman.cgi
Very cute and humorous. An on-line questionnaire for dogs to fill out to help them in selecting the appropriate human to live with.

Pet Horoscope

http://www.thepetchannel.com/horoscope.html
See what's in the stars for your mutt on a weekly basis. This is part of a large web site called the Pet Channel that contains an abundance of good information and resources.

DOG NAMING SITES

Dr. John's Dog Naming Web Site

http://indigo.ie/~jwilson/drjohn/
Contains 1,347 names to choose from. Click on each letter individually to bring up all names starting with that letter.

The Pet Names Pages

http://www.primenet.com/~meggie/petname.htm
A very decorative site that has everything and anything you would want to know about pet names. Names are categorized in several different links. You can look up names by types of pet, by color, by origin, etc. You can also add a name if you like. This is a fun site, even if you're not looking for a pet name.

PET LOST & FOUND SITES

Missing Pet Network

http://www.aphis.usda.gov/ac/anlost.htm
The Missing Pet Network (MPN) is a virtual linking of web sites throughout the country that are dedicated to helping reunite pet owners with missing or found pets. You can list a free classified ad for a lost or found pet, and may also post a pet's photo on-line.

Sherlock Bones

http://www.sherlockbones.com/html/
John Keane, aka Sherlock Bones, "Tracer of Missing Pets," is one of the country's leading authorities in the field of pet retrieval. His web site includes an advice area with helpful tips on how to protect your pet from being lost or stolen and how to keep your pet safe.

PET LOSS AND GRIEF

Virtual Pet Cemetery

http://www.lavamind.com/pet_menu.htm
Thousands of dog owners from around the world come to visit the Virtual Cemetery every day to read and share epitaphs. You can immortalize your mutt forever in cyberspace with a photo and story or poem. There is currently a small donation fee required; however, they say that even as little as $1 is acceptable.

Rainbow Bridge Tributes Pages
*http://rainbowbridge.tierranet.com/
bridge.htm*
This site opens with soothing music and nice graphics. There is no charge to memorialize your pet here, and they will accept photos and text via e-mail.

TRAVEL RELATED SITES

Travel Dog
http://www.traveldog.com/
Features extensive and up-to-date information on traveling with your dog. Pages include information on: Accommodations, dog camps, dog day-care, petsitters, pet transport, dog parks and beaches, and legal information.

Travel Web
http://www.travelweb.com/
This is not a pet-specific web site, but it has a searchable database that will find hotels that allow pets at your destination.

CYBER MUTTS

There are hundreds of mutt home pages from around the world with new ones being posted every day. Following are a few of the more interesting mutt sites I've run across.

Francis' Dog House
*http://www.caryn.com/francis-
index.html*
Francis, a great dane/lab mix, has quite a resourceful and entertaining web site. You can read her interesting life story, browse around the many dog links, or get your canine quote for the day from the "Quotes, Humor, Arts, and Literature" page. Among other things to see at Francis's house, are "Pick of the Litter" CDs; Francis's other web friends, and an entire page on the do's and don'ts for rollerblading with your dog—one of Francis's favorite things to do.

Pearlie the Wonder Dog
*http://www.artsnacks.com/pearlie/index.
html*
At Pearlie's site you can read about and see photos of her favorite activities, favorite foods, her dog and cat roommates, and other four-legged friends. But the most incredible thing on Pearlie's site is her life story, a must read.

Cassie's Three-legged Dog Club
*http://lark.cc.ukans.edu/~kurdavis/dogh
ome.html*
This is the first of its kind, club and web site for three-legged dogs and their owners. The canine founder of the club is a boxer mix, named Cassie, (short for Hopalong Cassidy) from Lawrence, Kansas. Features photos of Cassie, along with other three-legged dog club members. If you have a three-legged dog, your dog's photo and story can be posted on the site.

Misha's World Wide Woof!
*http://www.geocities.com/Heartland/
2376/*
Misha, a malamute/collie/shepherd mix, lives in Vancouver, Canada with Paul Parovish. Not only does she have one of the coolest mutt web sites, but she is also founder and president of "The Cool Mutts Club" web ring. And who says that mutts can't win "Best in Show"? Misha won the coveted title for the mixed-breed group on the Virtual Dog Show web site.

Max The Dog
http://www.maxthedog.com/
Read about the wacky adventures of Max, a big (that's 102 pounds big!) beautiful shepherd mix who lives in Westlake Village, California. Great graphics on this site, including milk-bone and paw print backgrounds. See Max's puppy photo album, meet some of his marvelous mutt friends, or read some of his favorite dog quotes.

ANNUAL EVENTS CALENDAR

There are numerous pet-related events and special observance days throughout the year that welcome dogs and animals of all types to participate. This section includes several events primarily for mutts but every type of dog is usually welcome to participate.

Participating in these events will put you in good company with fellow dog lovers, and will give you the opportunity to be involved in some worthy causes to benefit animals in need.

Events are listed in order by month. In most cases exact dates for events are not listed since they will occur on different dates each year. To find out event dates, times, and locations, contact the organization listed a few months prior to the month of the event. Since there are literally thousands of dog and pet-related events throughout the United States, they can't all be included here. This section features a small sampling.

FEBRUARY

SPAY DAY USA
Doris Day Animal League
227 Massachusetts Ave., NE #100
Washington, DC 20002
(202) 546-1761
A special observance day held on the last Tuesday of February to address the tragedy of pet overpopulation. Through various events and celebrations, people are encouraged to take responsibility for having one cat or dog spayed or neutered, whether it is his/her own, a friend's, or a shelter animal. For an event in your area, to learn more about Spay Day, or to report your participation, call: (888) SPAYDAY.

NATIONAL PET THEFT AWARENESS DAY
This day usually coincides with Valentine's Day on February 14th, and was established to make the public aware of the horrible problem of pet theft in the United States. Pets are stolen, sometimes from their own backyards, by people who sell them to medical research labs, or for other abusive purposes.

MARCH

GENESIS AWARDS
The Ark Trust
5551 Balboa Blvd.
Encino, CA 91316
(818) 501-2275
http://www.arktrust.org.
An annual event that honors outstanding individuals in the major media and artistic community whose journalistic integrity has increased public awareness of animal issues. Usually held at the Beverly Hilton Hotel in Beverly Hills, and also taped for later broadcast on Discovery's Animal Planet.

APRIL

PREVENT A LITTER MONTH

April marks the the onset of mating season for dogs and cats. Please spay and neuter your pets.

MAY

BE KIND TO ANIMALS WEEK
American Humane Association
63 Inverness Drive East
Englewood, CO 80112-5117
(800) 227-4645
http://www.americanhumane.org.
Always the first full week in May, the American Humane Association's "Be Kind to Animals Week" celebrates the bond between humans and animals. Contact your local animal shelter to find out how they are planning to celebrate.

Held in conjunction with this event is the "Be Kind to Animals Kid Contest," which recognizes children between the ages of six and thirteen who have shown extraordinary acts of kindness towards animals. For more information on Be Kind to Animals Week or the Kid Contest, contact American Humane Association.

ADOPTATHON
North Shore Animal League
25 Davis Ave.
Port Washington, NY 11050
(516) 883-7575
http://www.nsal.org
Adoptathon is a lifesaving weekend in the first week of May when animal organizations around the world join together to find a home for each and every pet. Participating shelters stay open longer hours during this weekend in an effort to place as many pets as possible in loving homes. To find a participating shelter or organization in your area, contact North Shore Animal League.

BIG DOGS GREAT L.A. DOG WALK
SPCA/LA
5026 W. Jefferson Blvd.
Lost Angeles, CA 90016
(888) SPCA-LA1
http://www.spcaLA.org
A 5K walk co-sponsored by Big Dogs Sportswear, around beautiful Griffith Park in Los Angeles.

DOG WALK AGAINST CANCER
American Cancer Society
19 West 56th Ave.
New York, NY 10019-3984
(212) 237-3872
http://www.dogswalk.com
A dog walk-athon to raise money for the fight against human and animal cancer. The American Cancer Society donates a portion of the proceeds to the Donaldson-Atwood Cancer Clinic at The Animal Medical Center in New York.

MUTT SHOW
Houston SPCA
900 Parkway Drive
Houston, TX 77024
(713) 869-8227
An annual salute to mutts. Only mixed breed dogs are allowed to participate. Ribbons and cash prizes are awarded for categories including: "Shortest Tail," "Shaggiest Dog," "Face Only a Mother Could Love," and "Longest Ears." Winners in these categories compete in the "Mr. and Mrs. Mutt" competition.

MUTT STRUT
Texas Animal Rescue League
P.O. Box 294375
Lewisville, TX 75029
(972) 420-0641
Dog walk and run to raise funds for animals at the Rescue League. Other activities include a dog wash and dip, and dog contests.

PET FAIR & MUTT SHOW
Scarborough Animal Centre
Centennial Community Recreation Ctr.
1967 Ellesmere Road
Scarborough, Ontario, Canada MlH 2X4
(416) 396-7387
First week of May. A 5K dog walk and show to benefit the Animal Centre. Mutt show follows the walk. Dog owners can enter dogs in seven fun categories, including "Mutt of the Year."

STRUT YOUR MUTT
Best Friends Animal Sanctuary
http://www.bestfriends.org
Well over a thousand people and their pets participate in this popular annual event that includes a dog walk and several fun contests afterwards.

JUNE

DAY OF THE MUTT
Sorocana, Brazil
In 1984, the city of Sorocana (fifty miles from Sao Paulo) declared the first Sunday of June as the "Day of the Mutt." On this day, dogs of unknown heritage are honored with a "Miss Mongrel" beauty contest, a dog biscuit reception, and other events.

ANIMAL WINGDING
San Francisco SPCA
2500 16th Street
San Francisco, CA 94103
(415) 554-3096
http://www.sfspca.org
A flotilla of people, animals, and vehicles march and ride down eight city blocks around the SF/SPCA. Pledges are collected to benefit animals at the SPCA. Features a street fair with pet products, arts and crafts, music, entertainment, and doggy demos.

SPRING MUTT MARCH
Michigan Humane Society
7401 Chrysler Drive
Detroit, MI 48211
(313) 872-3400
http://www.michiganhumane.org/
Take a one or five-mile stroll and help benefit animals at the humane society.

WAR DOG MEMORIAL
Hartsdale Pet Cemetery
75 North Central Avenue
Hartsdale, NY 10530
(800) 375-5234
http://www.petcem.com
Never forgotten, the hero canines of war are honored every Memorial Day at Hartsdale's War Dog Memorial monument. A special service is held complete with firing detail and a wreath laid on the monument. Hundreds of people attend this heartfelt service each year.

JULY

FREEDOM FESTIVAL
ALL-AMERICAN DOG SHOW
Vandenburgh Humane Society
P.O. Box 6711
Evansville, IN 47719
(812) 426-2563
This fun event is specifically for mutts. Each dog who enters is officially registered as an "All-American," and receives a certificate featuring its closest ancestry. Every dog wins a prize, and the top awards go to the first place: "All-American Dog," the second place:" Most Patriotic Canine Companion," and the third place: "Red, White, and Blue Mention."

AUGUST

NATIONAL HOMELESS ANIMALS DAY AND CANDLELIGHT VIGIL
International Society for Animal Rights
965 Griffin Pond Road
Clarks Summit, PA 18411
(806) 655-4336
e-mail: ISAR@aol.com
In 1992, the ISAR conceived this special day to raise awareness of the plight of homeless animals. Marked by candlelight vigils, this event is observed throughout the United States, Canada, and abroad on the third Saturday in August. Contact your local shelter or humane society to find out about events in your area. You can write ISAR for a free Vigil information packet.

MUTTFEST
Amarillo, Texas SPCA
800 W. 3rd Ave.
Amarillo, TX 79116
(806) 374-0704
Held at Sam Houston Park in Amarillo, Texas, Muttfest features live entertainment; search and rescue dog demonstrations; a doggie decathlon and several dog contests including: "Pet/Owner Look-Aike" and "Waggiest Tail." The afternoon ends with the crowning of "King" and "Queen Mutt," who are presented with royal crowns and capes.

SEPTEMBER

MUTT STRUT
Washington Humane Society
7319 Georgia Ave. N.W.
Washington, D.C. 20012
(202) 723-5730
An annual "Celebration of the Mixed Breed Dog," this event is just for mutts. Fun contests include: "Best Trick Dog," "Dog/Owner Look-Alike," and "Most Puzzling Parentage." T-shirts and buttons bearing the message "Mutts: Best of All Breeds" are available at the event.

NATIONAL PET MEMORIAL DAY
In 1986, the International Association of Pet Cemeteries declared the second Sunday of each September as a day of remembrance for beloved pets who have passed on. Several pet cemeteries around the country honor this day by holding "open-houses" and special memorial ceremonies.

FALL MUTT MARCH
Michigan Humane Society
7401 Chrysler Drive
Detroit, MI 48211
(313) 872-3400
http://www.michiganhumane.org/
Take a one or five-mile stroll and help benefit animals at the humane society.

SCRUFFTS
London RSPCA
Kym Reynolds
Causeway, Horsham
West Sussex, England RH12 1HG
011-44-1403 223264
http://www.rspca.org.uk
"Scruffts" is the Royal Society for the Prevention of Cruelty to Animal's (RSPCA) event to find the non-pedigree "Dog of the Year." The event is a spoof on the world renowned "Crufts" purebred dog show in England, much like our Westminster dog show in New York.

An estimated 10,000 mongrels (British term of endearment for mutt) compete in regional competitions across England and Wales. Sixty finalists then compete at the Scruffts final in early September.

NATIONAL DOG WEEK
Observed during the second week of September to show appreciation for the extraordinary relationship between humans and their canine companions. Check with your local shelter or humane society for events in your area.

OCTOBER

ADOPT A DOG MONTH

Established by the American Humane Association to encourage people to adopt dogs well before the holidays and *not* to give them as gifts.

ASPCA DOG WALK

ASPCA
424 East 92nd Street
New York, NY 10128-6804
(212) 876-7708
http://www.aspca.org
A one, two, or four-mile walk with or without a canine companion through Central Park in New York. Prizes are awarded for people bringing in the most pledges for the walk.

BLESSING OF THE ANIMALS

This special event is celebrated in conjunction with the Feast Day of St. Francis of Assisi, Patron Saint of Animals. Animal blessing events are held around the country in conjunction with various places of worship. Check with your local church, synagogue, or other place of worship for a celebration in your area.

The largest known blessing event in the United States is held at the Cathedral of St. John the Divine in New York City. An estimated 7,000 people and pets gather each year for this event.

WALK FOR THE ANIMALS
Helen Woodward Animal Center
P.O. Box 64
Rancho Santa Fe, CA 92067
(619) 756-0613
http://www.animalcenter.org/
Started in 1991, this event has grown into one of the largest animal events in Southern California. Animals of all shapes and sizes are welcome to participate with their human companions in a stroll through horse country.

NOVEMBER

HOUSTON SPCA MUTT STRUT

900 Portway Drive
Houston, TX 77024
(713) 869-7722
http://www.neosoft.com/~hspca/
A leisurely two-mile walk along Buffalo Bayou with your favorite canine friend. After the Strut there are Pet Fest activities and a Frisbee Dog Contest.

NATIONAL ANIMAL SHELTER AWARENESS WEEK

The first week in November is a time to show appreciation for all of the hard work and ongoing efforts put forth by animal shelters and humane societies to help homeless and needy animals.

STRUT YOUR MUTT
Clark County Nevada Parks & Rec.
P.O. Box 557110
Las Vegas, NV 89155-7110
(702) 455-8206
A non-traditional show for mixed and purebreds alike. Fun contests include: "Mutt Maze," "Silly Dog Tricks," "Puppy Love," "Howl at the Moon," "Hot Dog Fetch," and "Frisbee Frenzy."

DECEMBER

TREE LIGHTING
Hartsdale Pet Cemetery
75 North Central Avenue
Hartsdale, NY 10530
(800) 375-5234
http://www.petcem.com/
Each year the cemetery holds a special tree-lighting ceremony adjacent to its front gate. Plotholders and visitors are asked to bring offerings of pet food and supplies that are donated in their names to animal shelters in the area.

PRODUCTS, GIFTS, & MISCELLANEOUS

This section features resources for mutt-specific specialty items as well as general products, gifts, and services of interest to all dog lovers.

MUTT MEMENTOS

Annie May's Pet Hair Bears
2245 E. Colorado Blvd.
Box 104-163
Pasadena, CA
(818) 793-1070

For an everlasting memento of your mutt, you can save brushings or clippings from your dog's fur to be hand-spun into an original seven-inch keepsake teddy bear, created by award-winning fiber artist, Annie May Marshall. Handcrafting each bear is a five-hour process from "fur to finish." Prices range between $50 and $70. Clean brushed, shed, or cut groomed fur, a minimum of two inches in length is required.

For a free sample of your pet's yarn send a big handful of you pet's fur along with a legal-sized stamped envelope to the address above. Five percent of all proceeds go to Canine Companions for Independence, a national organization that provides service dogs for the deaf and disabled.

Mutt Tags and Keychains
I.D. Technology
117 Nelson Road
Baltimore, MD 21208
(410) 602-1911
http://www.id-technology.com

Your dog can show off the fact that he is of blended heritage by sporting a "100% Pure Mutt" dog tag, pictured above.

Tell the world that you're a proud mutt owner! Custom made just for readers of this book, you can order a stainless steel keychain (pictured above right) with your dog's name and photo, and an inscription that reads: "My M.U.T.T. (Most Unique Totally Terrific) DOG." Custom keychains are $17.95 each (or two for $27.95) plus $2 S&H."100% Pure Mutt" dog tags are $6.95 including S&H.

Pet Driver's License and Tags
Chloe Cards
1118 13th St., Dept. 25-B
Boulder, CO 80302
(888) 245-6388
http://www.concentric.net/~chloecrd

This looks just like the real thing! The actual size of a driver's license, laminated and in full-color featuring your pet's photo. Available for every state in the U.S. Issued by the PMV (Pet Motor Vehicles) Department.

A fun item to show family and friends, and a great way to keep your pet's information with you at all times. You can choose from: a wallet card, I.D. tag license for your dog to wear, a key chain, carrier/luggage tag, or digital file. $10.95 per item, plus tax, S&H. Printable order forms available at web site.

Mutt Mad Money
Kansas Bank Note Company
P.O. Box 360
Fredonia, KS 66736
(316) 378-3026
Put your money where your mutt is with personalized bank checks featuring your dog's photo. For a one-time artwork charge of $25, you can order 200 checks for $12 plus S&H. The cost actually works out to be less than many banks charge for checks. Contact Kansas Bank Note Company for ordering details.

Picture Your Mutt
Envision Publishing
P.O. Box 702925
Dallas, TX 75370
(888) IMAGIN-8
http://www.web2.airmail.net/jei/envision.html
Take your pick of a twelve-month laminated wall calendar featuring up to thirty special events of your choice printed on the calendar; a pack of ten customized greeting cards; or a custom screensaver with ten scans, all featuring your dog's photos.

GIFT ITEMS

Digital Dog Poster
San Francisco SPCA
2500 Sixteenth Street
San Francisco, CA 94103
(415) 554-3000
http://www.sfspca.org
This clever poster lists the dog's vital parts labeled in computer lingo. For example, the dog's ears are "dual floppies." More than thirty features listed. A "Computa Cat" version is also available. Full-sized posters are $12 each, plus $4.95 S&H per address. All proceeds benefit the SF/SPCA.

Match With Your Mutt
Le Pret Pet
20710 S. Leapwood Ave., Suite G
Carson, CA 90746
(800) 765-1376
Matching clothes for you and your dog, featuring mock turtleneck, Henley and T-shirt styles, with various prints. Call for pricing and ordering information.

Party in a Box, Party Animals
130 Skyline Drive Suite 132
Ringwood, NJ 07456
(800) 56-PARTY
Everything you need to throw a party for your dog. The "Party Pack" includes invitations, decorations, menu items,

refreshments, safety tips, games, party hats, bandannas, and doggy bags. Five percent of profits are donated to animal welfare organizations.

Paw-tographed Doggie Bandanna
Actors and Others for Animals
P.O. Box 33473
Granada Hills, CA 91394
(818) 755-6045
e-mail: aoa@a-service.com
Adorn your dog with a red bandanna bearing the paw prints of six famous canines, three of which are mutts: Beethoven, Benji, Dryfus, Eddie, Lassie, and Murray. One of several fundraising items sold by this nonprofit organization to help fund their many programs for animals in need. $9.50 (Incl. S&H)

Three Dog Bakery
1627 Main Street, 7th Floor
Kansas City, MO 64108
(800) 4-TREATS
(for orders or to receive a "Dogalog")
(888) 555-3647
(for bakery locations)
http://www.threedog.com
All natural treats for dogs that look so good you'll want to eat them yourself! Everything from "Bag o' Beagles" to "Snickerpoodles" can be found at this "canine confectionary and mecca for mutts." Call for a bakery location in your area or to receive a free "Dogalog," or visit their web site to see the latest treats available.

What's in the Cards for Your Mutt?
Pet Owner's Tarot Deck Company
P.O. Box 5661
Santa Monica, CA 90409
(800) 482-4733
See what the future holds for your dog with a thirty-two-card full-color tarot deck designed specially for pet owners.

MISCELLANEOUS

Contests

All American Pet Photo Contest
Fox Photo, Inc.
955 Marconi Drive
Alpharetta, GA 30005
(800) 955-9653
Annual contest for amateur photographers only. Enter as many photos of your dog as you wish. Cash prizes from $100 to $1,000. Call for contest deadline.

Dog Calendar Contest
Workman Publishing
Grand Central Station
P.O. Box 3927
New York, NY 10163
(212) 254-5900
http://www. workman.com
Each year 365 dogs are chosen to grace the pages of the popular 365 Dogs desktop calendar. Filled with quirky anecdotes, real-life stories, memorable quotes, and full-color photos. Photos are judged on their ability to set the tone for the day. Contact Workman Publishing for complete contest rules and deadlines.

Hero Dog of the Year
Ken-L Ration Dog Food
Reward Dog Hero of the Year
P.O. Box 1370
Barrington, IL 60611
Is there a heroic mutt or dog in your community who has gone to extraordinary lengths to assist someone in need? If so, then Reward wants to hear from you. For complete guidelines, send a

self-addressed, stamped business-size envelope to "Hero Dog Guidelines" at the above address.

David Letterman's Stupid Pet Tricks
(888) 738-8745
Does your dog perform any outstanding "stupid-pet-tricks?" Call the hotline number above and leave a detailed voice message explaining the trick(s) your dog does. If it sounds promising to the pet trick coordinator for the show, you will be contacted to see a videotape. If they like what they see, your dog could be the next stupid-pet-trick superstar.

Hotlines

The following hotlines are listed in alphabetical order, not by category.

Behavioral/Training Problem Hotline
American Dog Trainers Network
(212) 727-7257
A free helpline sponsored by the American Dog Trainers Network. Covers all aspects of information pertaining to dogs and offers referrals to a wide variety of dog-related professionals, services, and organizations. The helpline's hours of operation are between 1PM and 3PM (EST), seven days a week.

Lost and Found Hotline
Lost Pets: (900) 535-1515
($1.95 per minute)
Found Pets: (800) 755-8111
(no charge)
This is a 24-hour national hotline tracking system, sponsored by the American Humane Association and U.S. Sprint.

Low Cost Spay/Neuter Referral Line
SPAY/USA
(800) 248-SPAY
Call Monday through Friday, 9AM to 5PM for referrals of low cost spay/neuter facilities in your area.

National Animal Poison
Control Center
(800) 548-2423 ($30 per call)
or (900) 680-0000 ($20 for first 5 minutes, $2.95 each additional)
This hotline is located at the College of Veterinary Medicine, at the University of Illinois, and is staffed by actual veterinarians. The cost may seem a bit steep, but when your dog's life is on the line, it's a small price to pay.

National Disaster Assistance
United Animal Nations
P.O. Box 188890
Sacramento, CA 95818
(916) 429-2457
National emergency rescue program to help animals in crisis due to natural disaster situations such as floods, fires, hurricanes, etc. Volunteer training programs are offered in major cities across the United States for those interested in learning animal rescue procedures.

Pet Identification

Never let your dog or cat go without wearing some form of I.D. Thousands of pets are euthanized each year due to lack of identification. Described below are the two most common I.D. methods available.

• **Collar Tags** - This is the most commonly used form of I.D. Avoid using "S-hooks," as they are not as secure as round hooks. Many retailers and other pet-related facilities now have an instant pet I.D. machine available for you to have tags made while you wait.

• **Microchip** - A small chip implanted by injection under the pet's skin that contains a special code number. The code number is linked by computer to your pet's name, address, and phone number. Most animal shelters scan all incoming pets for microchip I.D.

Pet Loss Counseling Hotlines

Chicago Veterinary Medical Assoc.
(708) 603-3994
Leave a voice mail message and they will return your call from 7 PM to 9 PM CST. Toll calls will be returned collect.

Michigan State University
(517) 432-2696
Tues., Thurs. 6:30 PM to 9:30 PM EST.

Pet Friends
(800) 404-PETS
(609) 667-1717 (local South NJ calls)
Long distance calls returned collect.

Pet Loss Foundation
1312 French Road, Ste. A23
Depew, NY 14043
(513) 932-2270

University of California - Davis
(916) 752-4200
Mon. to Fri., 6:30 PM to 9:30 PM PST.

University of Florida
(904) 392-4700
Mon. to Fri., 7 PM to 9 PM EST.

Other Products and Services

Dog Gone Device
Sanjo Pet Products
(800) 368-7303
Never leave home without your mutt—that is if he or she is under twenty pounds. This is a backpack-style dog carrier that doubles as an automobile safety seat.

K-9 Cart Company
P.O. Box 160-639
Big Sky, MT 59716
(800) 578-6960
Specially designed custom wheelchairs to enable paraplegic or otherwise disabled dogs and cats to be mobile.

Pet Psychic
Lydia Hiby
P.O. Box 282
Sunland, CA 91040
(818) 365-4647
For answers to everything you always wanted to know about your dog, nationally known pet psychic, Lydia Hiby, can help. Featured on television, radio shows, and print media internationally, and author of *Conversations with Animals*. Phone consultations and seminars are available.

Pawsway
P.O. Box 764
Glenview, IL 60025-0764
(610) 644-6624
Ramps for mature or handicapped dogs to help them get up and down stairs, on and off beds, etc.

Veterinary Pet Insurance
4175 E. La Palma Ave.
Anaheim, CA 92807
(714) 996-2311
A pet health insurance plan that partially pays for office calls, prescriptions, treatments, surgery, and hospitalization.

Recommended Reading

MUTT BOOKS

Book of the Mixed Breed Dog by Andrew Prentis, Kay White. Barrons.

Cool Mutts by J.C. Suares, Helene D. Campbell. Stewart, Tabori and Chang.

Just Mutts: A Tribute to the Rogues of Dogdom by Steve Smith, Gene Hill. Willow Creek Press.

Mutts by Julie Mars. Miniature edition, Andrews & McMeel.

Mutts: America's Dogs by Brian Kilcommons, Michael Capuzzo. Warner Books.

The Mixed Breed: An Owner's Guide to a Happy Healthy Pet by Jeannette Stark. Howell Book House.

Zak: The One of a Kind Dog by Jane Lidz. Harry Abrams.

GENERAL DOG/PET BOOKS

Animals as Teachers and Healers: True Stories and Reflections by Susan Chernak McElroy. Ballantine Books.

Animals as Guides to the Soul by Susan Chernak McElroy. Ballantine Books.

Amazing But True Dog Tales by Bruce Nash. Andrews & McMeel.

Caring for Your Older Dog by Christopher C. Pinney. Barrons.

Circles of Compassion by Elaine Sichel. Voice and Vision.

Conversations with Animals by Lydia Hiby, Bonnie Weintraub. NewSage Press.

Dogs and Their Women by Barbara Cohen, Louise Taylor. Little, Brown.

Dog's Best Friend: Annals of the Dog-Human Relationship by Mark Derr. Henry Holt.

Dog Heralding: The Official Collection of Canine Coat of Arms by Mia Martin. Howell Book House.

Dogs Never Lie About Love: Reflections on the Emotional World of Dogs by Jeffrey Moussaieff Masson. Random House.

Dogs Who Came to Stay by George Pitcher. NAL/Dutton.

Food Pets Die For by Ann N. Martin. NewSage Press.

Found Dogs by Elise Lufkin, Diana Walker. Howell Book House.

Love, Miracles and Animal Healing by Dr. Alan M. Schoen. Simon and Schuster.

Out of Harm's Way by Terri Crisp, Samantha Glen. Pocket Books.

The Dog Who Loved Too Much by Nicholas H. Dodman. Bantam Books
The Dog Who Rescues Cats: The True Story of Ginny by Philip Gonzalez,
    Lenore Fleischer. HarperCollins.
The Lost History of the Canine Race: Our 15,000-Year Love Affair with Dogs
    by Mary Elizabeth Thurston. Andrews & McMeel.
War Dogs: Canines in Combat by Mike Lemish. Brasseys.
277 Secrets Your Dog Wants You to Know by Paulette Cooper. Ten Speed Press.

PET LOSS

Children and Pet Loss by Gary Kurz.
Cold Noses at the Pearly Gates by Gary Kurz.
Dog Heaven by Cynthia Rylant. (Reading level: Ages 4-8.) Scholastic Trade.
Pet Loss: A Spiritual Guide by Eleanor L. Harris. Llewellyn.

TRAVELING WITH YOUR DOG

Dog Lover's Companion by various authors. Foghorn Press.
Take Your Pet Too! by Heather M. Walters. MCE Publishing.
Mobil Travel Guide: On the Road With Your Pet. Fodor Travel.
Vacationing with Your Pet by Eileen Barish. Pet Friendly.

Index

ABOUT THE AUTHOR

A lifelong animal lover and advocate, Karen Derrico has become a strong voice for needy and homeless pets through her writing. Karen's publishing work on behalf of animals has earned her acclaim and recognition in broadcast and print, including: *The L.A. Times, Orange County Register,* and radio talk shows nationally.

Karen was editor and publisher for *Pet Gazette Magazine* and *The Pet Lover's Directory,* and has also written freelance articles for several animal related publications. She currently lives in Northern Virginia with her husband and son and her two lovable mutts.

Karen is currently compiling photos, stories, and information on anything unusual relating to dogs in the United States for an upcoming project. For submission guidelines, send a SASE to: Karen Derrico, P.O. Box 3468, Fairfax, VA 22038-3468.

OTHER BOOKS ON ANIMALS FROM NEWSAGE PRESS

Conversations with Animals:
Cherished Messages and Memories as Told by an Animal Communicator
by Lydia Hiby with Bonnie S. Weintraub
▼

Dancer on The Grass: True Stories About Horses and People
by Teresa tsimmu Martino
▼

The Wolf, the Woman, the Wilderness: A True Story of Returning Home
by Teresa tsimmu Martino
▼

Food Pets Die For: Shocking Facts About Pet Food
by Ann N. Martin
Foreword by Dr. Michael W. Fox
▼

Eating with Conscience: The Bioethics of Food
by Dr. Michael W. Fox
▼

Learning from Eagle, Living with Coyote
by Teresa tsimmu Martino

For more information on these and other books by NewSage Press,
visit our website http://www.teleport.com/~newsage. Or contact NewSage Press at:
PO Box 607 Troutdale, OR 97060-0607 (503) 695-221 • Fax (503) 695-5406

Hammond's Choice

A Marty Fenton Mystery Novel

Bob Cohen

Brandylane Publishers, Inc.
Richmond, Virginia

ISBN: 1-883911-79-6
         978-1-883911-79-9

Library of Congress Control Number: 2008921451

Brandylane Publishers, Inc.
Richmond, Virginia
brandylanepublishers.com

For

Robert Dunford and Joel Silverman

and

to the sweet memory of Jim Victor